Birgit Kasimirski
Englische Grammatik

Birgit Kasimirski

Englische Grammatik

Regeln, Beispiele, Übungen
für ein fehlerfreies Englisch

Anaconda

Penguin Random House Verlagsgruppe FSC® N001967

Die Deutsche Nationalbibliothek verzeichnet diese Publikation
in der Deutschen Nationalbibliografie; detaillierte bibliografische Daten
sind im Internet unter http://dnb.d-nb.de abrufbar.

© 2017, 2021 by Anaconda Verlag, einem Unternehmen
der Penguin Random House Verlagsgruppe GmbH,
Neumarkter Straße 28, 81673 München
Alle Rechte vorbehalten.
Umschlagmotiv und -gestaltung: Olaf Schumacher
Satz und Layout: Andreas Paqué, www.paque.de
Druck und Bindung: PBtisk s.r.o., Příbram
ISBN 978-3-7306-0317-8
www.anacondaverlag.de

Inhalt

To Carol and David from Malvern,
(not quite) Middle England.
Thanks for making me part of your family.
And to Dirk, Neela, Emil.

Noch ein Englisch-Grammatikbuch?

„Sprache ist Kleidung der Gedanken."
Samuel Johnson, englischer Schriftsteller

Sprachkompetenz kann man nicht von der Stange kaufen. Aber man kann es den Lernenden einfach(er) machen. Tatsächlich gibt es bereits unzählige Bücher zur englischen Grammatik. Englisch ist und bleibt gerade in unserer Zeit der Globalisierung wichtig, daher besteht ein laufender Bedarf, die Sprache auf neue Art und Weise zu lehren und lernen.

Seit mehr als zehn Jahren helfe ich Schülern und Erwachsenen, ihr Englisch zu verbessern, nicht als Lehrerin an einer Schule, sondern in einem privaten Umfeld und als Trainerin und Coach. Über die Jahre habe ich meine eigene Lehrmethode mit einem starken Fokus auf Praxisnähe und Anwendbarkeit entwickelt. Mit diesem Blick schaue ich auch auf die Lernenden: Was brauchen sie wirklich, was nicht unbedingt?

Praktikerin bin ich deshalb, weil ich Englisch in England gelernt habe – während meiner Arbeit in einem Übersetzerbüro und für kleinere Firmen, die den Austausch von Studenten aus den USA organisierten. Von April 1994 bis Dezember 1995 lebte ich die meiste Zeit in und mit englischen Familien zusammen in Worcester, Leeds, Malvern und London. Im anschließenden Anglistikstudium in Deutschland lernte ich zwar viel über Landeskunde, Literatur und Linguistik im akademischen Sinne, aber über gesprochene Sprache und praktische Grammatik nicht viel wesentlich Neues.

Während meiner Arbeit mit Englischlernenden ist über die Jahre ein Bild der englischen Grammatik in meinem Kopf entstanden: Englisch, das sind klare, übersichtliche Anwendungen für jede Zeitform und wiederkehrende, logische Strukturen. Dieses Bild habe ich versucht, mit diesem Buch auf Papier zu bringen.

Tipps zur Nutzung

Der große Vorteil vom Lernen außerhalb der Schule ist die Freiheit, selbst zu bestimmen und auszuwählen, was für einen interessant und relevant ist. Jeder Lernende einer Sprache weiß zudem, wie viel Zeit er investieren kann oder will. Lernfortschritte sind daher immer individuell.

Dieses Buch kann als Nachschlagewerk dienen oder dazu, die gesamte Grammatik zu wiederholen. Ebenso kann es immer mal wieder zur Hand genommen werden, um Ausdrücke oder Redewendungen anzusehen oder Übungen zu machen. Auf dieser Grundlage kann jeder im eigenen Tempo Vokabeln und Wortschatz ausbauen.

Mein Tipp ist: Schauen Sie sich den Überblick auf S. 21–23 und das Inhaltsverzeichnis an und entscheiden Sie, was Sie am meisten interessiert bzw. auf was Sie persönlich sofort eine Antwort haben möchten, und beginnen Sie dort.

TEIL EINS
Vorarbeiten

Einleitung

Eine Anekdote: Eine Freundin von mir spricht im Arbeitsumfeld seit vielen Jahren im In- und Ausland Englisch. Vor Kurzem fragte ich sie gezielt nach einem Tempus und erhielt die abenteuerliche Antwort: PRESENT-CONDITIONAL FUTURE (nein, diese Zeit gibt es nicht!). Da kam mir ein schönes Bild vor Augen: ein Würfelbecher mit allen Zeiten, die lustig hinausgewürfelt werden – völlig wahllos miteinander vermischt. Vielleicht erkennen Sie sich wieder?

Wie bei so vielen Dingen macht Lernen Spaß, wenn sich schnell Erfolge einstellen. Sprachen sind komplex, aber durch eine regelmäßige Anwendung gewöhnt sich unser Gehirn rasch an die neuen Strukturen. Die Gelegenheiten, mit Englisch in Berührung zu kommen, sind hierzulande vielfältig. Die Sprache begegnet uns täglich und überall: in der Musik, in Schriftzügen im öffentlichen Raum, in der Werbung, bei Namen. Es wäre schade, diese Gelegenheiten nicht zu nutzen. Wie wäre es beispielsweise mit fünf neuen Vokabeln täglich? Englischlernen in den persönlichen Alltag einzubauen macht Spaß.

Selbsteinschätzung (EU-Referenzrahmen)

Viele Lernende einer Sprache schätzen sich schlechter ein, als sie sind. Viele verfügen über gute Kenntnisse und befinden sich wahrscheinlich auf einem guten Fortgeschrittenenniveau, was dem europäischen Referenzrahmen Level A2 oder B1 entspricht. Lernende auf Level B2 oder C1 sind in der Lage, frei sprechend ihre Gedanken in den richtigen Zeiten wiederzugeben und verfügen über einen umfangreichen Sprachwortschatz.

Die Selbsteinschätzung ist wichtig für die Auswahl von Lehrbüchern, aber auch um zu wissen, wo man steht. Der gemeinsame europäische Referenzrahmen (GER) wurde 2001 vom Europarat eingeführt, um die verschiedenen europäischen Sprachzertifikate vergleichbar zu machen. Es gibt sechs Kompetenzabstufungen:

A1 – Anfänger

A2 – Grundlegende Kenntnisse

B1 – Fortgeschrittene Sprachverwendung

B2 – Selbständige Sprachverwendung

C1 – Fachkundige Sprachkenntnisse

C2 – Annähernd muttersprachliche Kenntnisse

Auf meiner Homepage www.birgitkasimirski.de finden Sie einen Link zu einem kostenlosen Einstufungstest.

Grammatikalische Grundbegriffe

„Etwa die Hälfte aller Fremdwörter
kann man vermeiden; man soll es auch tun …"
Kurt Tucholsky, Journalist und Schriftsteller

Eine Grammatik enthält zwangsläufig Fremdwörter. Meistens hat man sie schon mal gehört, aber die Bedeutung ist nicht mehr klar. Ganz ohne geht es nicht, deshalb nachstehend eine Auflistung von Begriffen aus der englischen Grammatik mit verständlichen Erläuterungen und Beispielen.

Aussagesatz

Positiver Satz, in dem keine Verneinung vorkommt; keine Frage.
Paul geht jeden Morgen um sieben Uhr zur Arbeit.
Paul goes to work every morning at 7 o'clock.

Continuous (= Progressive)

Bezeichnet immer eine VERLAUFSFORM des Verbs mit der Endung -ing. In manchen Lehrbüchern wird von CONTINUOUS gesprochen, in anderen von PROGRESSIVE, daher denken viele, es handle sich um unterschiedliche Zeiten. Tatsächlich bezeichnen die beiden Begriffe ein und dasselbe.
We are having a big party and you are invited.
They were running very fast.
I had been learning all afternoon.

Fragesatz

Es wird eine Frage formuliert.
Did you find the film interesting?
Were you happy in those days?
Are you hungry?

Gerundium

Die Substantivierung des Verbs. Aus einem Verb wird ein Hauptwort.
Im Deutschen großgeschrieben und häufig mit *das* vor dem Verb:

laufen   *das* Laufen

Im Englischen erhält das Verb die Endung -ing. Anders als beim
CONTINUOUS (das auch mit der Endung -ing gebildet wird) steht
das Gerundium alleine, ohne eine Form von to be:

to run   Running is fun.

Hilfsverb

Verben können in einem Satz entweder alleine stehen, dann sind sie
Vollverben. Wenn sie allerdings in Verbindung mit einem anderen
Verb zur Bildung einer Form gebraucht werden, dann sind sie Hilfs-
verben (siehe auch VOLLVERB). In einigen Zeitformen braucht man
Hilfsverben, um die Form überhaupt bilden zu können:

SIMPLE PRESENT

Do you like swimming?

do = Hilfsverb   like = Vollverb

PRESENT PERFECT

Have you seen mother?

have = Hilfsverb   seen = Vollverb

Imperativ

Befehlsform – die Form unterscheidet sich im Englischen nicht vom
INFINITIV.

Geh und hol die Tasche!

Go and get the bag!

Infinitiv (Grundform des Verbs)

Jedes Verb hat eine GRUNDFORM = INFINITIV, also eine Ausgangs-
form, von der aus alle Veränderungen in den verschiedenen Zeiten
vorgenommen werden (Konjugation). Vor der Grundform des Verbs
steht im Englischen in der Regel to.
Deutsch: gehen, laufen, rennen
Englisch: to go, to walk, to run

Komparativ

Vergleichsform des Adjektivs. Lässt sich gut merken über das englische Wort für vergleichen = to compare.
Louis is older than Marcus.

Konditional

Beschreibt eine Bedingung. Wenn A passiert, dann folgt daraus B. Im
Englischen sind das Konditional die if-Sätze.
If it rains, we will not be able to have our picnic.
I would leave the country too if there was war.

Modalverben

Drücken eine Fähigkeit, eine Erlaubnis oder einen Wunsch aus:
kann, darf, muss, soll. Auf die englischen Modalverben folgt immer
ein INFINITIV und sie können nicht in alle Zeiten gesetzt werden,
hierfür gibt es dann Ersatzformen.

Modalverb	Ersatzform
can	be able to
must	have to
should	be supposed to

Objekt

Der englische Satzbau ist strenger geregelt als der deutsche, er basiert auf dem Prinzip: SPO – *Subjekt, Prädikat, Objekt*. Das Subjekt ist eine Person oder Sache, die etwas tut, das Prädikat ist ein Verb, ein Objekt kann eine Person, ein Gegenstand oder ein Tier sein. Nach dem Objekt fragt man mit wen, wem oder was?

I brush my teeth.

Susan likes Tom.

Past Participle (Partizip Perfekt)

Das PARTIZIP PERFEKT ist die 3. FORM eines Verbs (siehe Darstellung unten). Regelmäßige Verben haben in der 2. und 3. FORM immer die Endung -ed. Verbtabellen existieren für die 2. und 3. FORM der unregelmäßigen Verben.

1. FORM = INFINITIV	2. FORM = SIMPLE PAST	3. FORM = PARTIZIP PERFEKT
Regelmäßige Verben:		
to rain	rained	rained
to laugh	laughed	laughed
Unregelmäßige Verben:		
to go	went	gone
to see	saw	seen

Possessivpronomen

Pronomen ersetzen Hauptwörter:

das Haus	= es	the house = it
der Mann	= er	the man = he

Possessivpronomen zeigen an, wem oder zu wem etwas gehört.

possessiv = besitzanzeigend, to possess = *besitzen*

das Haus des Mannes	= sein Haus	his house
die Frisur der Frau	= ihre Frisur	her haircut

Prädikat

Das ist immer das Verb innerhalb eines Satzes.

Progressive (siehe unter Continuous)

Relativpronomen

Relativsätze sind Nebensätze, die durch bestimmte Wörter, in diesem Fall Pronomen, eingeleitet werden. Die Wörter, die einen Nebensatz einleiten, heißen Relativpronomen.

The man, who lives next door, is very nice.

I wanted to tell mom about my exam which I passed.

Signalwörter

Die Verwendung bestimmter Wörter innerhalb eines Satzes hat zur Folge, dass unbedingt eine bestimmte Zeitform verwendet werden muss, etwa PRESENT PERFECT bei den Wörtern since und for (wenn diese *seit* bedeuten). Für diese Zeit sind since und for Signalwörter.

I have worked in this company for seven months now.

Subjekt

Jeder Satz hat ein Subjekt, also eine Person, eine Sache oder ein Sachverhalt, die/der in dem Satz etwas tut oder bewirkt.

I built a house.

A storm damaged the house.

Tense

Das englische Wort für „grammatikalische Zeitform". Der Begriff wird häufig hinter die einzelnen Zeiten gesetzt, beispielsweise SIMPLE PRESENT TENSE, SIMPLE PAST TENSE. Die Erfahrung zeigt: Jeder (neue) Begriff verunsichert die Lernenden (ist das wieder eine andere Zeit?). Vereinfacht handelt es sich schlicht um SIMPLE PRESENT und SIMPLE PAST.

Verb

Ein Verb gehört zum „Satzminimum" – ohne Verb gibt es keinen vollständigen Satz.

to see, to feel, to walk

Verbenliste

Die englische Grammatik unterscheidet zwischen REGELMÄSSIGEN und UNREGELMÄSSIGEN Verben. Regelmäßigkeit bedeutet, dass die Verben in der 2. und 3. FORM in der Regel die Endung -ed erhalten:

to walk – walked – walked   to rain – rained – rained

Unregelmäßige Verben dagegen weichen von der Regel ab. Für sie gibt es eigene Wortformen. Hierfür existieren Listen, die immer drei Formen enthalten, den INFINITIV, das SIMPLE PAST und das PARTIZIP PERFEKT.

1. FORM	2. FORM	3. FORM
INFINITIV	SIMPLE PAST	PARTIZIP PERFEKT
to go	went	gone
to see	saw	seen

Verneinung

Sätze, die eine negative Aussage enthalten, also Sätze mit not (nicht), die den Sinn ins Gegenteil verkehren.

Ich gehe heute *nicht* ins Fitness-Studio.

I do not go to the fitness club today.

Vollverb

Ein Verb, das in einem Satz allein das Prädikat bilden kann. Im Gegensatz zu Hilfsverben: to be, to do, to have, will oder Modalverben: can, must, will. Hilfsverben werden in Verbindung mit einem anderen Verb z. B. zur Bildung von Frage oder Verneinung gebraucht. Beispiele:

be als Vollverb: You are great.
be als Hilfsverb: Is she watching TV?

do als Vollverb: I do the washing.
do als Hilfsverb: I do not go to the theatre.

Zustandsverben

Zustandsverben bezeichnen keine TÄTIGKEIT, sondern einen (Geis-
tes-) ZUSTAND. Die Unterscheidung ist von Bedeutung, da Zustandsverben in der Regel nicht in die Verlaufsform (CONTINUOUS
= PROGRESSIVE) gesetzt werden.

Beispiele: agree, be, like, hate, know, need, promise, realize,
remember, see

Hilfsmittel + Lerntipps

Für das Sprachenlernen im Allgemeinen gilt: 30 Prozent Wissen
kann ein Lehrer vermitteln, etwa 70 Prozent muss der Lernende sich
selbst erarbeiten. Wie viel Zeit und Energie ein Lernender (außerhalb der Schule) darauf verwendet, ist sehr unterschiedlich. Im Gegensatz zu früher stehen heute über das Internet hervorragende Mittel zur Verfügung, die Zeit sparen und sich dazu eignen, auch mal
zwischendurch Übungen aufzurufen. Hier ein paar Hilfsmittel fürs
Englischlernen und allgemeine Lerntipps.

Wenn wenig Zeit ist

Kurzfilme auf YouTube anschauen (unter fünf Minuten):

Monty Python's Flying Circus – Football
        (www.youtube.com/watch?v = ur5fGSBsfq8)

Monty Python's Flying Circus – The Parrot Sketch
        (www.youtube.com/watch?v = npjOSLCR2hE)

Nespresso Werbung – George Clooney verhandelt mit John Malkovich
        (www.youtube.com/watch?v = sVoA4sT5W3M)

Look Up – A rhyming word film for an online generation.
        (www.youtube.com/watch?v = Z7dLU6fk9QY)

Die Kombination aus Sehen und Hören kommt einer Unterhaltung am nächsten. Im Unterricht kommt diese Art zu lernen sehr gut an und hat sich als sehr effektiv erwiesen. Alternativ kann man auf Online-Plattformen gezielt Grammatikübungen machen. Viele Plattformen bieten diese Übungen kostenfrei an, beispielsweise:

www.englisch-hilfen.de/exercises_list/alle_grammar.htm
www.ego4u.de/de/cram-up/tests

Wenn mehr Zeit ist

Sich Spielfilme in Originalfassung anzusehen, ist eine der besten Übungen, um das Sprachverständnis zu erhöhen – im Optimalfall sogar mit Untertiteln. Dann werden Sehen + Hören + Lesen trainiert. Das ist zwar anstrengender, bringt aber mehr Fortschritte. Alternativ kann man englische Texte lesen, ein englisches Buch oder Magazine (z. B. BBC News oder Spotlight). Das geht auch online:

www.bbc.com/news
www.spotlight-online.de

Wer etwas für seinen Wortschatz tun will, macht sich die Mühe, beim Lesen jede unbekannte Vokabel nachzuschlagen (auch das geht heute über online-Wörterbücher oder Apps viel schneller als früher). Diese Mühe wird durch einen größeren Wortschatz belohnt.

Generell

sollte man alle Möglichkeiten wahrnehmen, Englisch zu sprechen, und sich dann einfach mal trauen. Sicher ist erstens: Die meisten englischen Muttersprachler sprechen keine Fremdsprache, sie haben daher fast immer Respekt vor einem. Zweitens: Menschen anderer (nicht-englischsprachiger) Nationalität sprechen nicht unbedingt besseres Englisch. Optimal ist ein Aufenthalt in England oder einem anderen englischsprachigen Land mit Kontakt zu Landsleuten.

Zertifikate

Hat man einmal angefangen, Englisch zu lernen, lohnt sich die Überlegung, den Lebenslauf mit einer Qualifikation aufzubessern, etwa durch ein Zertifikat der Universität Cambridge. Zertifikate gibt es für jede Kompetenzstufe. Die Prüfungen finden regelmäßig in den größeren Städten statt.

Informationen unter www.cambridgeenglish.org/de/
(oder auf meiner Homepage www.birgitkasimirski.de).

Lerngruppen

Lerngruppen mit dem Ziel, Konversation zu betreiben, sind eine gute Möglichkeit, innerhalb kurzer Zeit Fortschritte zu machen. Eine Möglichkeit ist es, zum Beispiel über Aushänge oder Foren Gleichgesinnte zu finden und sich in 3er- oder 4er-Gruppen in regelmäßigem Abstand zum Sprechen zu treffen – idealerweise ist eine Person dabei, die das Ganze professionell unterstützen kann.

Überblick englische Zeiten – das Grundgerüst

Die Zeiten sind das Grundgerüst der Sprache. Wenn man sicher weiß, wann welche Zeit in welcher Form angewendet wird, ist man gewappnet für das Sprechen. Stimmt die Grammatik, dann kann man am Wortschatz arbeiten und ihn durch Praxis weiter ausbauen. Wer sich sicher auf diesem Gerüst bewegt, kann gutes Englisch sprechen. In der unten angeführten Reihenfolge werden die Zeiten im Folgenden erklärt. Auf den ersten Blick scheint eine unübersichtliche Anzahl englischer Zeiten zu existieren. Insgesamt sind es (lediglich) ACHT verschiedene Zeiten, die GEGENWART, VERGANGENHEIT und ZUKUNFT ausdrücken. Sich dies bewusst zu machen, kann dabei helfen, dass die Grammatik nicht mehr so groß und umfangreich erscheint. Wie die unten stehende Tabelle verdeutlicht, kommen ei-

nige Zeiten zweimal vor, beispielsweise PRESENT PERFECT (GE-
GENWART + VERGANGENHEIT) oder PRESENT CONTINUOUS
(GEGENWART + ZUKUNFT). Wichtig ist es für Schüler, hier zu erkennen: Weiß ich diese acht Zeiten anzuwenden, bin ich grundsätzlich in der Lage, die meisten Situationen zu beschreiben.

1   SIMPLE PRESENT

2   PRESENT CONTINUOUS

3   PRESENT PERFECT

4   SIMPLE PAST

5   PAST PERFECT

6   PAST CONTINUOUS

7   WILL FUTURE

8   GOING TO FUTURE

Gegenwart

+ UNTERFORMEN

1 SIMPLE PRESENT	
2 PRESENT CONTINUOUS	
3 PRESENT PERFECT	PRESENT PERFECT CONTINUOUS

Vergangenheit

3 PRESENT PERFECT	PRESENT PERFECT CONTINUOUS
4 SIMPLE PAST	
5 PAST PERFECT	PAST PERFECT CONTINUOUS
6 PAST CONTINUOUS	

Zukunft

7 WILL FUTURE	WILL BE DOING WILL HAVE DONE FUTURE
8 GOING TO FUTURE	
2 PRESENT CONTINUOUS FUTURE	
1 SIMPLE PRESENT FUTURE	

Die nachfolgende Grafik auf S. 24 stellt eine Zeitschiene dar, von der VERGANGENHEIT (links unten) zur ZUKUNFT (rechts oben). Zeiten, die zweimal vorkommen, sind unterstrichen. Nicht in der Grafik aufgeführt sind die Unterformen. Sie werden im Grammatikteil TEIL ZWEI – DIE ZEITEN erläutert.

Die Grafik auf S. 25 zeigt die Zeiten in der Anwendung. In TEIL DREI – DAMIT WIRD ES KOMPLETT werden alle weiteren Aspekte der englischen Grammatik erklärt, die für eine korrekte Anwendung der englischen Sprache notwendig sind.

Zeitschiene

Zukunft

WILL FUTURE

GOING TO FUTURE

PRESENT CONTINUOUS FUTURE

SIMPLE PRESENT FUTURE

Gegenwart

SIMPLE PRESENT

PRESENT CONTINUOUS

PRESENT PERFECT

Vergangenheit

PRESENT PERFECT

SIMPLE PAST

PAST PERFECT

PAST CONTINUOUS

Zeiten angewendet

Future

… will join you …

… is going to study after school …

… is coming tomorrow …

… starts at 8 pm …

Present

… looks nice …

… is working right now …

… have been to the shop …

Past

… has known her since …

… went home …

… had left before …

… was watching TV when …

Die Beugung der englischen Verben

Die Verben der englischen Grammatik verändern sich immer in bestimmter Weise. Andere als diese Veränderungen gibt es nicht.

I.
Jedes Verb hat einen INFINITIV = GRUNDFORM = die 1. FORM. In der Regel steht vor dem Infinitiv ein to.
to go
to walk
to cry

II.
Im SIMPLE PRESENT erhält das Verb ein s, wenn he, she oder it verwendet werden.
he goes
she talks
it rains

III.
(Fast) jedes Verb kann in die VERLAUFSFORM = CONTINUOUS gesetzt werden.
Bei einer Zeit im CONTINUOUS muss das Verb in der ing-Form stehen und es gibt immer eine Form von to be.
I am thinking of you.
She is driving a new car.
They are living in a big house.
They were feeling rather worried.
You have been dreaming all night.
He will have been dreaming something nice.

IV.
Jedes Verb (Ausnahme Modalverben) hat eine 2. FORM = SIMPLE
PAST. Unregelmäßige Verben haben Formen, die man lernen muss
(siehe VERBENLISTE), regelmäßige Verben enden immer auf -ed.

INFINITIV	2. FORM	
to go	went	unregelmäßig
to see	saw	unregelmäßig
to rain	rained	regelmäßig
to live	lived	regelmäßig

V.
JEDES VERB (Ausnahme Modalverben) hat eine 3. FORM = PARTI-
ZIP PERFEKT. Auch hier gilt bei unregelmäßigen Verben die Liste,
bei regelmäßigen die Endung -ed. Kommt die 3. FORM vor, muss
IMMER auch have oder has oder eine Form von to be stehen.

INFINITIV	have/has/to be	3. FORM	
to go	you have	gone	unregelmäßig
to see	she has	seen	unregelmäßig
to carry	they are	carried	regelmäßig
to live	I have	lived	regelmäßig
to place	it was	placed	regelmäßig

VI.

Die Verbenliste wird immer in drei Spalten dargestellt. In diesem Buch werden diese als 1. FORM, 2. FORM und 3. FORM bezeichnet.

1. FORM		2. FORM	3. FORM
INFINITIV		SIMPLE PAST	PARTIZIP PERFEKT
Verwendung: SIMPLE PRESENT WILL FUTURE GOING TO FUTURE nach MODALVERBEN IMPERATIV		Verwendung: SIMPLE PAST	Verwendung: PRESENT PERFECT PAST PERFECT WILL HAVE DONE FUTURE PASSIV
to go	U	went	gone
to like	R	liked	liked
to find	U	found	found
to rain	R	rained	rained
to drive	U	drove	driven
to snow	R	snowed	snowed
to taste	R	tasted	tasted
to steal	U	stole	stolen

U = unregelmäßiges Verb
R = regelmäßiges Verb

HINWEIS: In den Verbenlisten werden in der Regel nur die unregelmäßigen Verben derart aufgelistet – bei den regelmäßigen ist klar: Die Endung lautet immer -ed.

Aufbau des zweiten Teils

Bei jeder Zeitform wird im Folgenden erklärt, wann die Zeit verwendet wird, was häufig falsch gemacht wird, worauf man achten sollte und wie man Aussage, Verneinung und Frage richtig bildet. Danach folgen jeweils Zitate aus dem Sport, Beispielsätze und Redewendungen unter Verwendung der jeweiligen Zeit sowie Übungen. Die Lösungen stehen am Ende des Buches.

TIPP: Bei den Zitaten und Beispielsätzen kann jeder für sich den Gegencheck machen: Trifft zu, was als Kriterium für die Zeit gilt? Dieser kritische Blick verstärkt den Lernerfolg.

HINWEIS: Im Buch werden keine Vokabeln aufgeführt. Das ist Teil des effektiven Lernens: Unbekannte Wörter sollen nachgeschlagen werden. Dank der Mittel, die heute zur Verfügung stehen (App und Internet), bedeutet das wenig Zeitaufwand bei hohem Lern-Effekt. Hingegen: Phrasen und Redewendungen werden auf Englisch und Deutsch aufgeführt.

In jedem Kapitel gibt es einen leeren Kasten für Notizen und offene Fragen, den man nutzen kann, um Unklarheiten gleich an Ort und Stelle festzuhalten.

TEIL ZWEI
Die Zeiten

Gegenwart
Simple Present

= einfache Gegenwart
Wird verwendet
1. für wiederholte Handlungen,
2. für allgemeine Aussagen,
3. für feststehende Handlungen in der Zukunft = Fahrpläne,
4. für aufeinanderfolgende Handlungen in der Gegenwart first, then …
5. für Anweisungen.

SIMPLE PRESENT wird verwendet, um auszudrücken, dass etwas REGELMÄSSIG, WIEDERKEHREND passiert, oder wenn etwas GENERELL gilt. Außerdem ist es eine Form der Zukunft, dann aber ausschließlich bei Fahrplänen (die in der Regel jeden Tag, also regelmäßig und generell gelten, siehe SIMPLE PRESENT FUTURE, S. 118).

TYPISCHE SITUATION: BESCHREIBUNG VON PERSONEN + SITUATIONEN
Im SIMPLE PRESENT werden Personen beschrieben: Wo lebt jemand? Wie lebt jemand? Was mag jemand? Sowie Ansichten, Vor-

lieben oder Meinungen: Welche Einstellung hat jemand, welche Hobbies?

Signalwörter (Beispiele)

every day, often, always, sometimes, never

> ❗ Mit dem SIMPLE PRESENT haben die meisten keine Schwierig-keiten, es wird nur manchmal zu häufig verwendet, also z. B. auch, wenn eigentlich etwas anderes (nichts Regelmäßiges, Ge-nerelles) ausgedrückt werden soll. Das Gute: Man wird dann verstanden, kann sich damit durchschlagen, es ist aber kein gu-tes Englisch. Zu Verständigungsschwierigkeiten kann es führen, wenn jemand sagt I go to my mother und damit meint, dass er jetzt dort hingeht, denn für den Engländer bedeutet es: „Ich be-suche meine Mutter regelmäßig."

> ❗ Die häufigsten FEHLER: Das -s bei he, she, it wird vergessen und do/does werden bei Verneinung und Frage nicht verwendet.

SIMPLE PRESENT bilden:

Aussage

Eine Aussage wird im SIMPLE PRESENT mit der GRUNDFORM DES VERBS = INFINITIV gebildet, jedoch bei he, she, it mit -s am Verb. In der Schule lernen die Kinder bereits: He, she, it das -s muss mit!

I live in Berlin.	generell	
You work as an English teacher.	generell	
My father believes in politics.	generell	he
My mother hates lazy people.	generell	she
The train leaves at 7 pm.	wiederkehrend	it
We study in evening classes.	wiederkehrend	
You like swimming, don't you?	generell	
First they feed the cats, then the dogs.	aufeinander folgende Handlung	

Infinitiv

he she it mit -s

> **!** Verben, die auf Zischlaute wie -s, -ss, -z, -ch enden, erhalten bei he, she, it die Endung -es für eine leichtere Aussprache, also watches und nicht watchs. Verben, die auf -y enden, erhalten die Endung -ies.

to watch	he watches
to catch	she catches
to fetch	it fetches
to fly	he flies
to dry	she dries
to cry	it cries

Verneinung

Bei der Verneinung im SIMPLE PRESENT wird das Hilfsverb do mit not + INFINITIV benötigt, bei he, she, it mit does + not. Im Deutschen heißt es: Ich lebe in Berlin. – Ich lebe *nicht* in Berlin. Im Englischen reicht das not allein nicht! Es gibt Lang- und Kurzformen, beide können gleichermaßen verwendet werden, in der Regel wird bei der Langform die Verneinung stärker betont.

	Lang-	Kurzform	
I	do not	don't	play the monkey in this piece!
You		don't	go to evening classes anymore.
He	does not		find it very funny at all.
She		doesn`t	usually get up very early.
It	does not		seem fair at all.
You		don't	get it, do you?
We		don't	get on well with the neighbours.
They	do not		like sports.

> ❗ BEACHTE: Bei does wandert das -s vom INFINITIV zum Hilfs-
> verb do und wird wegen der leichteren Aussprache zu -es.

She likes me.
s
She does not like me.

Frage

Auch die Frage braucht zwingend das Hilfsverb do/does, hier am
SATZANFANG + INFINITIV. Es kommt sehr oft vor, dass dieses vergessen wird. Manchmal wird versucht, aus dem Deutschen so zu
übersetzen: Like you water? You like water? Das versteht man zwar,
es ist grammatikalisch aber falsch. Richtig muss es heißen:

Do you like water?
Do I get tickets over there?
Do you find football interesting?
Does he have a lie in in the mornings?
Does she go to the hairdresser's every Monday?
Does it really cost 2,000 Euros?
Do you have brothers and sisters?
Do we start at 7 am like last week?
Do they get a new car every year?

Fragewörter

what	=	was
where	=	wo
when	=	wann
why	=	warum

how	=	wie
how much	=	wie viel
how many	=	wie viele
who	=	wer
whose	=	wessen
which	=	welche (bei Auswahl)

Fragewörter gehören grundsätzlich an den SATZANFANG, also noch vor do oder does.

What does it mean?

When do you usually play tennis?

Which table do you prefer, the one at the window or this one here?

Verneinte Frage

Es gibt die Möglichkeit, verneinte Fragen zu stellen – auf die man nur mit JA oder NEIN antworten kann. Hier wird in der Regel die KURZFORM verwendet:

Don't you look gorgeous?	Yes, of course.
Doesn't she play wonderfully.	Yes, she really does.
Don't we go this way?	No, we decided not to.
Don't they get on well?	Unfortunately not.

Simple Present in a nutshell

he, she, it = -s an das VERB

FRAGE und VERNEINUNG mit HILFVERB do und

das -s wandert ans Hilfsverb = does

NICHT: does + VERB + -s (= Doppel-S)

To be + to have

To be „sein" und to have „haben" erfüllen zwei Funktionen: Sie können als Vollverb und als Hilfverb gebraucht werden. To be wird ohne do/does bei Frage und Verneinung gebildet. Bei to have dagegen besteht die Wahl: mit oder ohne.

To be

I am	ich bin
you are	du bist
he, she, it is	er, sie, es ist
you are	ihr seid
we are	wir sind
they are	sie sind

Bildung von:

AUSSAGE	VERNEINUNG	FRAGE
I am young.	I am/'m not old.	Am I right?
You are great.	You are not/aren't a genius.	Are you mad?
He is a monster.	He is not/isn't a bad guy.	Is he really?
She is fun.	She is not/isn't boring.	Is she?
It is fantastic.	It is not/isn't magic.	Is it a miracle?
You are tired.	You are not/aren't awake.	Are you here?
We are knackered.	We are not/aren't fresh.	Are we OK?
They are out.	They are/aren't in.	Are they?

Have got + have

Für das besitzanzeigende „haben" können Sie have got oder have verwenden, es bleibt Ihnen überlassen. In manchen Büchern heißt es, have got müsse zur Kennzeichnung von Besitz, Beziehungen, Eigenschaften und Krankheiten verwendet werden, für alles andere gelte have. Andere Grammatiken machen keine Unterscheidung. Tatsächlich wird in England have got häufig verwendet. Wichtig ist:

Verwenden Sie have got, ist die Bildung von Verneinung und Frage eine andere, als wenn Sie nur have verwenden:

Have got

I have got a nice little house.
She has got beautiful hair.
Which hairdresser has she got?
They have got four children!

Verneinung

I haven't got a sister.
He hasn't got a sore throat.

Frage

Have you got a brother then?
Has she got a sore throat?

Have

Das besitzanzeigende „haben" have (ohne got) muss bei Verneinung und Frage mit dem Hilfsverb do/does gebildet werden.
I have a nice little house.
She has beautiful hair.
Which hairdresser has she?
They have four children!

Verneinung

I don't have a sister.
He doesn't have a sore throat.

Frage

Do you have a brother then?
Does she have a sore throat?

PRAXIS: Have kann man nicht immer durch have got ersetzen, zum Beispiel:

Ich hatte einen Unfall.   Wir hatten Fisch zu Mittag.
I had an accident.   We had fish for lunch.

To do

Das Verb to do „tun/machen" kommt im SIMPLE PRESENT in jeder FRAGE und VERNEINUNG als HILFSVERB vor, es kann im gleichen Satz aber auch *gleichzeitig* als VOLLVERB stehen:

Do als HILFSVERB + VOLLVERB in FRAGE und VERNEINUNG
I dont't do my homework on Fridays.
You don't do anything for me!
Does he do you a favour every now and then?
She does not do the washing up in our house.
It doesn't do what I want it to.
How do you do?
We don't do nice things at the weekend.
They do not do their homework on their own.

Do kann auch verwendet werden, um Aussagen zu verstärken und ihre Bedeutung für den Sprecher hervorzuheben:
I believe in the success of the project.
I do believe in the success of the project.   verstärkende Aussage
Und do kann als Platzhalter dienen für ein Verb, das vorher schon verwendet wurde und nicht wiederholt werden soll. Im Deutschen steht dann an dieser Stelle lediglich die Person: *Meine Schwester spielt kein Tennis, aber ich!* Im Englischen dagegen heißt es:
My sister doesn't play tennis, but I do.

Kurzantworten

Kurzantworten sind die korrespondierenden Erwiderungen auf geschlossene Fragen, also solche, auf die man nur mit ja, nein oder vielleicht antworten kann. Dabei gilt: Genauso wie die Frage gestellt wurde, so wird geantwortet:

Is she hungry perhaps?	Maybe she is.	No, she isn't.
Have you got time now?	I have indeed.	No, I haven't, sorry.
		(Achtung:
		Hier entfällt das got!)
Do you have anything		
to drink?	Yes, I do.	I'm afraid, I don't.
Are you sleeping?	Yes I am.	No, I am not.

Fragen, Unklarheiten, Notizen

Für die Sportfans –

SIMPLE PRESENT in FOOTBALL-NEWS

"Klopp wants his team to forget a record (...) EIGHT goals from corners this season – the highest in the Premier League – and 13 in total from set pieces, and instead use the 'power of Liverpool' to reach Wembley."

www.mirror.co.uk/sport/football/news

Beispielsätze Simple Present

My father works as a policeman.
I do not stay out long at night in the street after dark.
I find it strange when people say they don't like foreigners.
Every Monday my friend and I go for a walk.
When I am tired, I cannot stay up very late.
Sometimes we go to see a football match on a Saturday night.
Whenever I find the time, I sit down and read a paper.
My friend Sue doesn't think she is very clever. But I do.
Pink clothes don't do anything for you.
In other words, pink doesn't suit you.
Holger wants to come to England with us.
Do you ever go swimming at the weekend?
She finds it hard to understand how he could do that.
Does she do her homework straight after school?
I have got two sisters and one brother, she has only got one sister.
Does she have a pet? Has she got a pet?

Redewendungen Simple Present

A phrase often comes in handy.	ist nützlich
Peter looks up to Alan.	bewundert Alan
He absolutely drives me nuts!	Er bringt mich auf die Palme!
Too many cooks spoil the broth.	Zu viele Köche verderben den Brei.

It never rains but it pours.
Ein Unglück
    kommt selten allein.

All's well that ends well.
Ende gut, alles gut.

Little strokes fell big oaks.
Steter Tropfen höhlt den Stein.

This is not my cup of tea.
Das ist nichts für mich.

Lies have short legs.
Lügen haben kurze Beine.

Great minds think alike.
Zwei Dumme, ein Gedanke.

When in Rome,
    do as the Romans do.
sich anpassen

I do you a favour
einen Gefallen tun
    and get no thanks.
    ohne Erwiderung

Do you think we can do away
    with this?
Kann das weg?

Monkey see, monkey do.
nachäffen

Kids without toys
    make do with anything.
sich behelfen

At school the children
    make fun of me!
sich über jemanden lustig machen

They make good headway.
kommen gut voran

Tim and Tom
    make faces at each other.
Grimassen schneiden

They hardly make ends meet.
kommen finanziell
    kaum zurecht

Life is what you make it.
Jeder ist seines Glückes Schmied.

There is no fool like an old fool.
Alter schützt vor Torheit nicht.

Praxis

Hinweis zu den Übungen: Wenn Sie Vokabeln nicht kennen, schlagen Sie sie nach und sehen Sie es als Chance an, Ihren Wortschatz aktiv zu vergrößern – so funktioniert Lernfortschritt.

It's your turn
Übung 1

Sätze bilden mit SIMPLE PRESENT

a. Das Brot sieht lecker aus.

The bread looks delicious.

b. Er will nicht essen, es sei denn ich füttere ihn.

He doesn't eat, unless I feed him.

c. Spielen sie nicht immer mittwochs Schach?

Don't you play chess every wednesday?

d. Er kennt viele Gedichte auswendig.

He knows many poems by heart.

e. Vergisst deine Mutter manchmal etwas?

Does your mother forget things sometimes?

f. Welches Buch mag er am liebsten?

Which book does he like the most?

g. Wie gefällt dir meine neue Frisur?

How do you like my new hair ~~dress~~ style?

Übung 2

Mit BE + HAVE

a. Montags haben die Kinder Schule bis um halb zwei.

On monday, the kids have school until half past one.

b. Sie ist niemals pünktlich.

She is never in time.

c. Sie hat einen BMW und einen Porsche in der Garage.

She has a BMW and a Porsche in the garage.

d. Wir sind schon zufrieden, wenn die Sonne scheint.

We are already happy, if the sun shines

e. Mein Vater hat zwei Brüder und fünf Schwestern.

My father has two brothers and five sisters

f. Bin ich denn so spät?

Am I that late?

g. Hast du Zeit für einen dummen alten Mann wie mich?

Do you have time for a dumb old man like me?

h. Sie sind nicht mit dem zufrieden, was sie haben.

They are not happy with what they have

Übung 3

FRAGEN STELLEN mit und ohne FRAGEWORT

a. Ist sie aus New York?

Is she from NY?

b. Trifft sie sich später mit ihrem Freund?

_____

c. Haben wir jetzt zwei Hunde?

_____

d. Heißt ihr Ann und Cathy?

_____

e. Mögen die beiden Schach?

_____

f. Wann spielen Sie Tennis?

_____

g. Warum hat sie keinen Ehemann?

_____

Übung 4

SIMPLE PRESENT – S oder nicht?

We _____ (to live) in Berlin and _____ (to visit) our friends every day. My friend Ann _____ (not to live) in a big city. She _____ (to live) in a small town instead. There _____ (not to be) a lot to do at all. She _____ (not to go) to work every day, since she only _____ (to have) a part-time job. Anyway, I _____ (to be) not sad about it because this way she _____ (to be able) to meet me whenever she _____ (to want) to.

Present Continuous

= Verlaufsform der Gegenwart

Wird verwendet
1. bei Handlungen, die im Moment des Sprechens ablaufen,
2. um auszudrücken, dass man von etwas genervt ist,
3. bei Beschreibungen, was wir auf Fotos/Bildern sehen,
4. bei feststehenden Handlungen in naher Zukunft.

PRESENT CONTINUOUS (= PRESENT PROGRESSIVE) wird verwendet, wenn ausgedrückt werden soll, dass etwas im Moment des Sprechens passiert, also Tätigkeiten im Verlauf, daher auch die Bezeichnung „Verlaufsform". Häufig handelt es sich dabei um Handlungen oder Tätigkeiten, die über einen gewissen Zeitraum = Zeitspanne andauern. Es ist auch eine Form der Zukunft für Dinge, die fest geplant sind und sicher in naher Zukunft eintreffen werden.

TYPISCHE SITUATION: Darauf hinweisen, was man gerade tut!
Was machst du gerade? Woran arbeiten Sie gerade?

! In der Bildung finden Schüler diese Form in der Regel nicht schwierig. In der Anwendung ist sie den meisten nicht als Form der Zukunft bekannt, siehe PRESENT CONTINUOUS FUTURE, S. 115.

Signalwörter (Beispiele)
now, at the moment, Look! Listen!

PRESENT CONTINUOUS bilden:

Zeiten im CONTINUOUS (= PROGRESSIVE) haben immer ein Verb mit der Endung -ing. Das PRESENT CONTINUOUS braucht die Endung -ing in Verbindung mit einer Form von to be.

am/is/are + Verb + -ing

Aussage

Zu der ing-Endung des Verbs gehört für die Bildung des PRESENT CONTINUOUS immer eine Form von to be (Lang- oder Kurzform):

I am/'m sitting here, reading a book.

You are/'re playing beautifully!

He is/'s getting me the paper from the shop.

She is/'s vacuuming the living room. Can't you hear?

It is/'s pouring down with rain outside.

We are/'re walking round the Beacon.

You are/'re snoring. Wake up!

They are/'re laughing so loudly, I can't concentrate!

Verneinung

Hier wird einfach ein not eingefügt. Es können Lang- oder Kurzformen verwendet und auf diese Weise auch verneinte Fragen gestellt werden:

I am/'m not singing, are you deaf?

You are not/aren't cooking lunch by any chance?

He is not having a shower at the moment.

Isn't she working today?

It isn't snowing, for goodness sake.

We aren't flying, are you kidding!

You are not snoring, what a relief.

They aren't laughing, they are crying!

Frage

Die Form von to be tauscht den Platz mit dem SUBJEKT = PERSON
und steht jetzt am SATZANFANG:

In other words, you are asking: Am I working right now?
Are you sorting these things out?
Is he really trying something new?
Is she cutting with the large knife?
Is it raining right now?
Are we watching a film, you mean?
Are you sitting on the bus? I'll call later then.
Are they carrying their children?

Zur Bildung der ing-Form: Die Regel besagt, dass an einen INFINITIV
-ing angehängt wird. Ausnahme: Nach einem betonten Vokal (a, e, i,
o, u) wird ein einfacher Konsonant verdoppelt, und bei den meisten
Verben, die auf -e enden, entfällt dieses (weil es nicht gesprochen
wird):

to begin	beginning
to sit	sitting
to stop	stopping
to come	coming
to shame	shaming
to give	giving

Besondere Anwendungen

Immer bei Bildbeschreibungen
PRESENT CONTINUOUS wird generell verwendet, um Bilder zu beschreiben, um z. B. mitzuteilen, was auf einem Foto zu sehen ist. Es
ist, als passiere es im Moment des Betrachtens.

Look! In the photograph mom is looking really funny.
What a hat you are wearing!
This painting is wonderful, it is using such bright colours.
On the poster in my bedroom a girl is riding on a horse.

Zum Ausdruck bringen, dass man genervt ist

Mit PRESENT CONTINUOUS kann man auch ausdrücken, dass einem das Verhalten einer anderen Person nicht gefällt:

You are always throwing your clothes on the floor!

Das stört mich total.

ZUM VERGLEICH:

You always throw your clothes on the floor!

Eher neutral, es ist eben so.

The neighbour is always parking on my parking lot!

I am always forgetting my purse when leaving home!

Eigentlich sind es ja Dinge, die regelmäßig passieren (SIMPLE PRESENT), jetzt verändert sich der Ton: wie nervig!

Zustandsverben oder Statische Verben

PRESENT CONTINUOUS drückt also aus, dass etwas über einen bestimmten ZEITRAUM passiert. Das macht nicht bei allen Verben Sinn, beispielsweise bei DENKEN. I think bedeutet „ich denke, glaube". Der Satz: *Ich denke, das ist richtig,* beschreibt eine Geisteshaltung, einen momentanen Zustand. Sagt man dagegen: Quiet, I am thinking, wird mit dem CONTINUOUS betont, dass der Denkprozess gerade wichtig ist.

Verben, die in der Regel keine Tätigkeiten ausdrücken, stehen normalerweise nicht im CONTINUOUS. Diese Verben heißen ZU-STANDSVERBEN. Sie sind nicht dynamisch, sondern statisch, daher der Name. Sie betonen nicht etwas, das passiert, sondern etwas, das so ist. Dazu gehören auch die Verben der EMPFINDUNG: to feel, to smell, to hear, to see.

AUSNAHME: Will man ein solches Gefühl oder eine besondere Empfindung betonen, bedient man sich der VERLAUFSFORM auch für diese Verben! Noch ein HINWEIS: Manche Verben beschreiben manchmal einen Zustand, manchmal eine Tätigkeit:

I have	besitzen	I am having food	essen
I feel	Meinung	I am feeling well	Befinden
I see	verstehen	I am seeing	sehen
I think	glauben	I am thinking	nachdenken

Zustandsverben (Beispiele)

to agree	to fear	to be
to fit	to matter	to believe
to feel	to mean	to belong
to hate	to need	to care
to prefer	to depend	to hear
to dislike	to imagine	to realize

Wichtigkeit hervorheben

Also: Will jemand ein Gefühl hervorheben, kann er es betonen, indem er es gleichsam in die Länge zieht (CONTINUOUS):

How do you feel about it?
How are you (really) feeling about it?   Betonung

Mehr Beispiele:
You are a bad girl.
You are behaving very badly!   Betonung
She needs new glasses.
She is really needing help now!   Betonung
I care for you.
We are caring for our mother.   Betonung

Present Continuous in a nutshell

Immer eine Form von to be + Verb mit -ing
Zustandsverben in der Regel nicht mit -ing,
außer man will Wichtigkeit betonen oder
besondere Bedeutung hervorheben.

Fragen, Unklarheiten, Notizen

Für die Sportfans –

PRESENT CONTINUOUS in BOXING NEWS

"Meanwhile, David Haye is having a comeback against a Nobody on a TV channel that advertises itself as 'the home of witty banter'".
www.theguardian.com/sport/queensberry-rules-boxing-blog

Beispielsätze Present Continuous

My father is working at the moment.
I am having something to eat right now.
I am tired, I cannot stay up much longer.   Zustandsverb
Listen: This man is saying he does not like foreigners.
We are swimming today because it's Monday.
We are walking to the football match.
I am now finally sitting down, reading a paper.
Are you watching television again?
My friend Sue is thinking too much.   Genervtheit
They are feeling very sad after the film.
Are you driving home at the moment?

Redewendungen Present Continuous

What are you having?	Was nimmst du (zu essen)?
It is raining cats and dogs.	Es gießt wie aus Kübeln.
Hey, are you pulling my leg?	Nimmst du mich auf den Arm?
He is blowing his own trumpet!	Er lobt sich selbst.
He is getting away with it again.	Er kommt wieder ungeschoren davon.

Praxis

It's your turn
Übung 5

Sätze im PRESENT CONTINUOUS bilden

a. Sie sitzen gerade im Garten.

_____

b. Wir laufen, weil der Bus kommt.

_____

c. Ich telefoniere im Moment nicht.

_____

d. Auf dem Foto stehen wir gerade vor der Kirche.

_____

e. Im Moment macht sie gar nichts.

_____

f. Ruhe! Du machst eine Menge Lärm!

_____

g. Wie fühlst du dich?

_____

h. Schau, die Vögel trinken das Wasser.

_____

Übung 6

-ING oder nicht?

a. Ich glaube, der neue Kollege ist ziemlich nett.

_____

b. Sie versorgt ihre Mutter.

_____

c. Es macht mir etwas aus, wie es dir geht, weißt du!

_____

d. Glaubst du an irgendetwas?

_____

e. Das bedeutet uns sehr viel.

_____

f. In diesem Fall ist das nicht von Belang.

_____

g. Sie glauben nicht, dass er die Prüfung jetzt im Moment mitschreibt.

_____

h. Mir wird gerade erst bewusst, dass du verletzt bist.

_____

Zwischen Vergangenheit und Gegenwart
Present Perfect

= Bezug zwischen Gegenwart und Vergangenheit
Wird verwendet, wenn
1. ein Bezug zum oder eine Bedeutung für das Jetzt besteht,
2. etwas seit … anhält,
3. etwas aus der Vergangenheit noch nicht abgeschlossen ist.

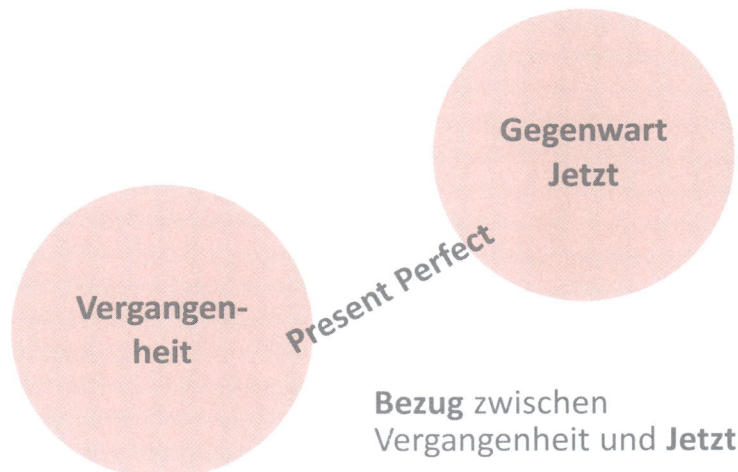

PRESENT PERFECT ist die schwierigste Form der englischen Grammatik. Manche verwenden sie gar nicht, viele verwenden sie falsch. Dieses Kapitel soll helfen, zu verstehen, warum PRESENT PERFECT wichtig ist und wie es gebildet und verwendet wird. Es gibt zwei Formen: PRESENT PERFECT (SIMPLE) und PRESENT PERFECT CONTINUOUS (VERLAUFSFORM).

Generell gilt: PRESENT PERFECT muss verwendet werden, wenn der Sprecher ausdrücken will, dass etwas zu einem Zeitpunkt in der

Vergangenheit begonnen hat und noch andauert, oder wenn er zum Ausdruck bringen will, dass es eine Bedeutung für das Jetzt, einen direkten Bezug zur Gegenwart gibt – zumindest für ihn also eine gefühlte Nähe zum Geschehen.

Manchmal ist diese Bedeutung wirklich nur subjektiv. Ob die Nähe besteht, ergibt sich aus dem Zusammenhang eines Gesprächs. Es gibt aber auch sichere Signale für oder gegen das PRESENT PERFECT.

> **!** Im Deutschen wird ein Bezug zwischen Vergangenheit und Gegenwart allein durch Zusätze wie Zeitangaben ausgedrückt, z. B. *seit gestern*. Dass es im Englischen hierfür eine eigene Zeit gibt, macht es schwierig für uns, das Konzept dahinter zu verstehen und die Zeit anzuwenden. Auch die Bildung bereitet Schwierigkeiten. Es braucht daher vor allem Übung. Tatsache ist: PRESENT PERFECT (+ PRESENT PERFECT CONTINUOUS) kommen im Englischen sehr häufig vor und sind wichtig, um gutes Englisch zu sprechen. Mein Tipp: auf die Zeit bewusst achten (in Radio Songs und geschriebenen Texten), sie wird irgendwann geläufig und geht in Fleisch und Blut über.

Signalwörter (Beispiele)
since, for, already, before, ever, never, so far, still not, yet

> **!** Ungeübte sollten sich einprägen: Immer wenn sie „jemals" oder „niemals" verwenden, steht PRESENT PERFECT!
>
> Ich war noch nie(mals)
> in Amerika.   I have never been to America.
> Warst du jemals da?   Have you ever been there?

Present Perfect bilden

Aussage

Um PRESENT PERFECT zu bilden, wird immer das Hilfsverb have
(oder has bei he, she, it) in Verbindung mit dem PARTIZIP PERFEKT
= 3. FORM des Verbs benötigt.

have oder has +
3. Form

| 1. FORM = INFINITIV | 2. FORM = SIMPLE PAST | 3. FORM = PARTIZIP PERFEKT |

1. FORM = INFINITIV	2. FORM = SIMPLE PAST	3. FORM = PARTIZIP PERFEKT
to build	built	built
to go	went	gone
to drive	drove	driven
to speak	spoke	spoken
to see	saw	seen

Beispielsätze

I	have	dreamt	of you.
You	have	played	chess.
He, she, it	has	slept	well.
We	have	had	a party.
You	have	been	ill.
They	have	come	home.

Verneinung + not

I	have	not	dreamt	of you!
You	have	not	played	fair.
He	has	not	got	the paper yet.
She	has	not	found	any shells.

Frage – have/has an den SATZANFANG

Have	I	dreamt	a bad dream?
Has	he	slept	in my bed tonight?
Have	you	been	to the doctor already?
Have	we	paid	yet?

Kurzformen

AUSSAGE	VERNEINUNG	
I've	haven't	dreamt this night at all.
You've	haven't	gone home.
He's	hasn't	seen her today.
She's	hasn't	found her purse.
It's	hasn't	hurt its leg.
We've	haven't	been to the doctor.
They've	haven't	smiled all day.

HINWEIS: Eine Kurzform mit Apostroph s kann also für is (he is) und auch für has (he has) stehen. Für alle möglichen Apostroph-Fälle siehe S. 143.

Present Perfect Continuous

= Verlaufsform des PRESENT PERFECT

Dass es hier eine Verlaufsform gibt, ist nur logisch, denn Handlungen, die vor einiger Zeit begonnen haben und noch andauern, sind zwangsläufig noch im VERLAUF. Trotzdem ist es für Lernende nicht einfach zu erkennen, wann PRESENT PERFECT SIMPLE steht und wann die VERLAUFSFORM. Hier die Unterscheidung: Beim PRE-SENT PERFECT SIMPLE wird eher betont, dass eine Handlung, ein Zustand beendet wurde und ein Ergebnis vorliegt. Beim PRESENT PERFECT CONTINUOUS liegt der Fokus auf einer Handlung, einem Zustand, der noch nicht beendet ist.

VERGLEICHE:

We have lived here since 2010.   SIMPLE
We have been living here since 2010.   CONTINUOUS

CONTINUOUS: Der Sprecher wohnt seit 2010 hier und immer noch. Zieht er jedoch gerade aus, ist SIMPLE die richtige Wahl.

We have come home.   SIMPLE
We have been coming home.   CONTINUOUS

Der erste Satz sagt, dass jemand (gerade) nach Hause gekommen ist (Ergebnis, er ist zu Hause). Der zweite Satz impliziert, dass dieses Nachhause-Kommen länger angedauert hat und sogar immer noch andauert. Das macht wenig Sinn! Es hängt also davon ab, welche Tätigkeit ausgeführt wird. Hier ist die einfache Form die richtige Wahl.

Present Perfect Continuous bilden
Aussage

PRESENT PERFECT CONTINUOUS wird immer mit der 3. FORM von to be = been in Verbindung mit have/has + einem Verb mit ing-Endung gebildet:

have/has + been + -ing

I	have	been	dreaming	of you all night.
You	have	been	playing	chess for three hours now.
He	has	been	living	with her since 2013.
She	has	been	cooking	all morning for us.
It	has	been	raining	without a break.
We	have	been	having	a wonderful time here!
You	have	been	feeling	rather ill, haven't you?
They	have	been	looking	for a car for ages.

Verneinung + not

have/has + not + been + catching

I	've not (haven't) been getting	any replies from you.
He	's not (hasn't) been sleeping	well.
You	've not been listening	I guess.
They	've not been looking	for a car.

Frage

Am SATZANFANG:

have/has + been + catching

Have I been snoring all night?

Has she been sitting here for two hours?

Have you been watching the programme?

Have they been cooking?

Present Perfect in a nutshell

have/has + 3. FORM

DIREKTE Bedeutung, Bezug zu JETZT

Kein Zeitpunkt genannt

NÄHE zum Geschehen

VERLAUFSFORM have + been + ing

Wann Present Perfect?

Da PRESENT PERFECT (SIMPLE + CONTINUOUS) fast allen Lernenden der englischen Sprache Schwierigkeiten bereitet, hier eine Auswahl von typischen Situationen, in denen diese Zeit in der Praxis gebraucht wird.

Alltagssituationen

Grundsätzliches: Ganz oft sprechen wir im Alltag über Dinge, die für uns als Sprecher JETZT von Bedeutung sind, die eine Verbindung zu HANDLUNGEN oder ZUSTÄNDEN haben, die in der Vergangenheit begonnen wurden bzw. ein Resultat aus diesen Handlungen oder Zuständen betreffen. Der Zeitpunkt in der Vergangenheit kann dabei länger zurückliegen oder gerade erst vergangen sein. Nochmal: Das ist für uns Deutsche grammatikalisch neu, denn wir haben keine eigene Zeit dafür.

Situation A

Andrew kommt nach Hause, niemand ist da. Er wundert sich, eigentlich müsste seine Mutter zu Hause sein. Da hört er das Türschloss. Die Mutter kommt herein. Andrew wird mit Sicherheit fragen:
Where have you been?
Mother: Sorry, I have just been next door to fetch some milk!
Es betrifft ihn JETZT (Zeitpunkt des Sprechens), dass die Mutter nicht da ist, weil sie vorher (Handlung in der Vergangenheit) weggegangen ist. SIMPLE, denn die Betonung liegt darauf, dass die Handlung beendet ist (Mutter ist wieder da).

Situation B

Marie ist vor fünf Minuten aus dem Haus gegangen. Sie hat ihre Tasche liegen gelassen. Ihre Mutter ruft sie auf dem Handy an:
You have left your bag!
Marie: Oh bother!

Es betrifft sie JETZT, weil sie die Tasche nicht mitgenommen hat (Handlung in der Vergangenheit). Bedeutung: Sie muss unter Umständen zurückkommen. SIMPLE, denn auch hier liegt der Fokus auf dem Ergebnis (Tasche liegt zu Hause).

Situation C
Robinsons besuchen Verwandte. Der Sohn macht einen müden Eindruck. Die Tante fragt:
What's the matter with Bob?
Father: Oh, he's just tired, he has played football all morning.
Etwas betrifft die Tante JETZT, sie kann sehen, dass etwas (Handlung in der Vergangenheit) ihn müde gemacht hat (Ursache, Wirkung, Bedeutung für JETZT). SIMPLE, denn der Fokus liegt auf dem Ergebnis (Neffe ist müde).

Gespräche: Wo wohnst du? Wo arbeitest du?
Wenn wir mit jemandem darüber reden, was wir beruflich machen und wo wir wohnen, benutzen wir meistens PRESENT PERFECT (SIMPLE oder CONTINUOUS), weil die Situation bzw. der Zustand des Wohnens bzw. Arbeitens noch andauert:

Gespräch A
Seit wann wohnt ihr hier?
We have been living here since 2005 – and you?
We have just moved here recently.
Die erste Familie wohnt seit 2005 hier und auch weiterhin, Betonung auf der Handlung, die andauert = CONTINUOUS. Die zweite Familie ist gerade hergezogen, Betonung des Ergebnisses einer Handlung = SIMPLE.

Gespräch B
Arbeitest du schon lange für diese Firma?
I have worked for the company for the last 20 years.
I have been working for them for the last 20 years.

Die erste Aussage betont ein Ergebnis = SIMPLE. Möglicherweise hat die Person aber gerade bei der Firma aufgehört. Die zweite Aussage betont die Handlung = CONTINUOUS. Sie arbeitet auch weiterhin dort. Es ist also weder das eine noch das andere „falsch". Vielmehr kommt es auf die Motivation des Sprechers an. Was zutrifft, ergibt sich oftmals nur aus dem weiteren Zusammenhang des Gesprächs.

Gespräche über Erfahrungen, z. B. Reisen + Freunde

Auch bei Gesprächen über das Reisen kommt sehr häufig PRESENT PERFECT vor, es sei denn, wir berichten über eine Reise, die in der Vergangenheit (BERICHTEN = abgeschlossene Handlungen ohne Bezug zu JETZT = SIMPLE PAST) stattfand und vorbei ist. Wenn wir jedoch darüber sprechen, wo wir schon überall waren oder genau das vom Gegenüber wissen wollen, ist immer auch „bis heute" JETZT gemeint. Deshalb kommt hier PRESENT PERFECT ins Spiel. Dasselbe gilt für Freunde, mit denen man JETZT immer noch befreundet ist.

Gespräch A

Have you ever been to the USA?
No, so far I haven't made it there!

Frage: Bist du jemals (in der Vergangenheit bis heute) dort gewesen? Betonung auf dem Ergebnis = SIMPLE.

Gespräch B

How long have you known each other?
I have known her for seven years.

Seit wann kennt ihr euch? Der Fragende geht davon aus, dass die beiden sich immer noch kennen und auch weiterhin befreundet sind. Die Antwort bedeutet: seitdem und jetzt immer noch. Hier wird ein Zustand betont, der anhält, jedoch gehört to know zu den Zustandsverben, die in der Regel nicht in eine Verlaufsform gesetzt werden, daher wird hier SIMPLE verwendet.

Nachrichten

Nachrichten werden regelmäßig im PRESENT PERFECT verfasst, denn die Neuigkeiten haben sich vor kurzem in der Vergangenheit ereignet und es liegt in der Natur der Sache, über Ergebnisse von Handlungen oder Zuständen zu berichtet, die JETZT neu, also wichtig sind für den Zuhörer oder Zuschauer.

Nachricht A

EU leaders holding late-night talks in Brussels have agreed to relocate tens of thousands of migrants who have arrived in Italy and Greece.
(BBC NEWS online, 26 June 2015) Betonung auf Ergebnissen von Handlungen = SIMPLE.

Nachricht B

Shell has said today the company will dismiss 200 of its 3000 workers on a US-drilling platform.
(BBC NEWS online, 26 June 2015) Betonung auf Ergebnissen von Handlungen = SIMPLE.

Nachricht C

A woman has collapsed today following a shooting in a shopping mall outside Birmingham. It has not yet been reported whether she was injured or not.
(BBC NEWS online, 26 June 2015) Betonung auf Ergebnissen von Handlungen = SIMPLE.

Nachricht D

The kite festival in Devon has seen over 4,000 visitors today on a sunny and warm day.
(BBC NEWS online, 26 June 2015) Betonung auf Ergebnissen von Handlungen = SIMPLE.

Nochmal: Alle Nachrichten sprechen von etwas, das zum Zeitpunkt der Veröffentlichung gerade erst passiert ist. Es sind Neuigkeiten für den Zuhörer und daher jetzt für ihn wichtig.

Present Perfect + Continuous gegenübergestellt

Continuous

She has <u>been</u> watching TV all day.
They have <u>been</u> looking for a new car for two weeks.
Beide Aussagen betonen die Handlung (Fernsehen schauen, Auto suchen), und diese sind zum Zeitpunkt des Sprechens noch nicht beendet.

Der gleiche Satz im Simple

She has watched TV all day.
They have looked for a new car for two weeks.
Hier betonen die Aussagen das Ergebnis und es wird ausgedrückt, dass die Handlungen Fernsehen schauen und Auto suchen beendet wurden.

Ein letztes Beispiel – die lieben Nachbarn

He has had troubles with his neighbour recently.
He has <u>been</u> having troubles with his neighbour ever since he moved here.
Auch hier wieder eine unterschiedliche Betonung der Aussagen: Im ersten Fall wird das Ergebnis betont (wegen des Streits ist das Verhältnis zum Nachbarn schlecht). Im zweiten Fall wird der Zustand betont und dass dieser nicht beendet ist (es gibt also immer noch Streit mit dem Nachbarn).

Daneben gibt es sichere Signale für PRESENT PERFECT
SINCE + FOR

since

for

= seit

Since und for in der Bedeutung von „seit" erfordern in der Regel das
PRESENT PERFECT. Denn mit PRESENT PERFECT sprechen wir
über Dinge, die andauern – von einem Zeitpunkt in der Vergangenheit bis JETZT. For ist außerdem eine Präposition, die auch in anderen Zusammenhängen vorkommt: He lived in London for ten years.
Hier bedeutet for aber nicht „seit", sondern „über einen Zeitraum
von". Es ist gut, wenn man sich folgendes angewöhnt: Verwendet
man since oder for in der Bedeutung von SEIT, dann IMMER mit
PRESENT PERFECT! Since wird verwendet, wenn ein ZEITPUNKT in
der Vergangenheit genannt wird, for steht für eine ZEITSPANNE.

SINCE für ZEITPUNKT in der Vergangenheit
last Monday, a year ago, 1996, the day I was born, on 5th July 2012,
last Christmas, winter 1989, the moment when we met, a few sec-
onds ago, our last holiday

FOR für ZEITSPANNE bis heute
two weeks, seven days, a long time, quite a while, ages, a few sec-
onds, more than two weeks, over a whole year, one term, all summer, half the holiday, a while

SINCE
We haven't seen them since last Monday.
We have known each other since we were little.

FOR

She has looked after her neighbour's dog for a week.

I haven't seen her for ages.

Warum Present Perfect so schwierig ist

Es sind manchmal nur kleine Änderungen, die bedingen, ob Sätze im PRESENT PERFECT oder SIMPLE PAST stehen müssen (S. 71).

Noch einmal zur Situation B auf S. 59, um zu verdeutlichen, wann kein PRESENT PERFECT verwendet wird:

Marie ist vor fünf Minuten aus dem Haus gegangen. Sie hat ihre Tasche liegen gelassen. Ihre Mutter ruft sie auf dem Handy an:

You have left your bag!

Marie: Oh bother!

Kurz darauf ruft Marie bei ihrer Arbeitsstelle an:

Sorry, I will be late, I have left my bag at home and have to return for it.

Es ist gerade passiert und die Information ist wichtig für die Arbeit JETZT. Betont wird das Resultat, die Tasche liegt zu Hause. Hinweis: Im Satz steht *keine* Zeitangabe.

Am Abend trifft sich Marie mit Freunden. Sie erzählt, was ihr passiert ist:

Can you believe it? This morning I forgot my bag when I left home and was late for work!

Hier berichtet Marie vom Morgen. In einigen Grammatiken wird dem Schüler für die Bildung von PRESENT PERFECT eben diese Hilfe angeboten, nämlich dass oft kein genauer Zeitpunkt in der Vergangenheit genannt wird und dass bei Nennung eines Zeitpunkts SIMPLE PAST verwendet wird. Das trifft häufig zu, aber darauf sollte man sich nicht verlassen. Das nachfolgende Kapitel führt alles Wissenswerte über die korrekte Bildung von SIMPLE PAST auf.

Für die Sportfans –

PRESENT PERFECT in FORMULAR 1-NEWS

"Mercedes have already established a 30-point lead at the top of the constructors' table, as they look to retain the title."

www.mirror.co.uk/sport/formula-1

Beispielsätze Present Perfect Simple

Hier wird das *Ergebnis* betont.

Sheila has lived in lots of different countries.

I have visited Italy before.

You can have the book. I have read it.

Have you ever been to Canada?

Workers have found remnants of a 200 year old building.

We have seen very little of John next door lately.

Have you settled in? – Not yet.

I have had enough of this.

(I have) been there, (I have) done that!   Alles schon gesehen.

Beispielsätze für Present Perfect Continuous

Hier wird die *Handlung* betont und sie ist noch nicht beendet!

We have <u>been</u> having a good time at the party.

I have <u>been</u> looking for Sheela all day. Where could she be?

It has <u>been</u> snowing all day.

She has <u>been</u> having troubles with the bank.

They have <u>been</u> waiting for ages and there is no result yet.

We have not <u>been</u> getting much support so far.

I have <u>been</u> wanting to go to Germany ever since I heard about it.

Praxis

It's your turn
Übung 7

Sätze bilden mit PRESENT PERFECT + CONTINUOUS

a. Wir sind erst vor kurzem hierher gezogen.

_____

b. Es ist 11 Uhr und sie ist immer noch nicht aufgestanden.

_____

c. Seit gestern habe ich sie nicht mehr gesehen.

_____

d. Dieses Jahr haben wir keinen Urlaub gebucht.

_____

e. Wir waren bereits dreimal in Canada.

_____

f. Hast du mir etwas vom Mittagessen aufgehoben?

_____

g. Seit wann arbeitest du schon für Paul?

_____

h. Wir fahren seit drei Wochen mit dem Schiff durchs Mittelmeer.

_____

Übung 8

Was passt? PRESENT PERFECT oder CONTINUOUS unterstreichen

a. If you have known/have been knowing this for days,
   why haven't you told/been telling me earlier?

b. He has had/has been having a good time at the camp so far.

c. We have seen/have been seeing much more of you since
   David has worked/has been working part-time.

d. I have told/have been telling you for weeks to buy the share.
   Now it's too late, the prices have gone/have been going up.

e. I have had/have been having a haircut, do you like it?

f. My father has had/has been having an argument with mom, and
   I have heard/have been hearing every single word.

g. Children, let's go outside, we have spoken/have been speaking
   all morning about math and you have behaved/have been behaving so well – that should do.

h. Have you seen/have you been seeing the movie? I think it's
   great!

Übung 9

Was passt? SIMPLE PRESENT
oder PRESENT PERFECT unterstreichen

a. Er fährt jede Woche einmal mit dem Rad zur Arbeit.
   He cycles/has cycled to work once a week.

b. Seit zwei Jahren fährt sie mit dem Auto zur Arbeit.
   She drives/has been driving to work by car for the last 2 years.

c. Sie gehen sehr oft ins Kino.
   They go/have gone to the cinema very often.

d. Er wohnt seit 1995 in England.

He lives/has been living in England since 1995.

e. Sie spielt schon sehr lange Gitarre.

She plays/has played the guitar for a very long time.

f. Sie übt jeden Tag eine Stunde.

She practices/has practiced an hour every day.

g. Wir kennen uns schon ewig.

We know/have known one another for a long time.

h. Immer wenn ich traurig bin, tröstet sie mich.

Whenever I am sad, she comforts/has comforted me.

Übung 10
PRESENT PERFECT

oder PRESENT PERFECT CONTINUOUS einsetzen

a. I (to call) _____ you for half an hour.

Where (you, to be) _____? And why are

your clothes so dirty?

b. I (to tidy) _____ up the shed in the garden.

c. (you, to find) _____ a box with old photos there?

I (to look) _____ for it for ages.

d. I (not to discover) _____ it yet, but

maybe I (not to look) _____ properly.

I (to come, just) _____ in to eat something.

e. I (not to cook) _____ anything yet

because I (to talk) _____ to our neighbour

for so long.

f. (you, to have) _____ a nice holiday?

I think you must (to have) _____ a lot

of sun judging by your tan.

g. Andrew should come outside now, he (to watch)

_____ this stupid programme all morning!

h. Susan, come on and hurry up! Anyway, what are you doing? –

I (to clean) _____ my teeth as you

(to tell) _____ me I should do!

Übung 11
Sätze erweitern mit PRESENT PERFECT

a. I love her. (I met her)

Beispiel: I have loved her since I met her.

b. She is living on her own. (her husband died)

c. He is confined to a wheelchair. (he had an accident)

d. We have been living here. (three months)

e. Does she have a cat? (how long)

_____

f. She puts much effort into it. (she got the order)

_____

g. He sees the doctor regularly. (his daughter told him)

_____

h. You miss me. (I left)

_____

Vergangenheit
Simple Past

= einfache (abgeschlossene) Vergangenheit
Wird verwendet, wenn
1. der Zeitpunkt des Geschehens klar in der Vergangenheit liegt
   und das Geschehen vorbei ist,
2. über (zeitlich) abgeschlossene Ereignisse berichtet wird.

SIMPLE PAST = einfache Vergangenheit wird immer dann verwendet, wenn wir über etwas sprechen, das einmalig oder mehrmals in der Vergangenheit passiert ist, häufig berichten wir also über etwas – und sei es noch so kurz her, z. B. a minute ago. Man kann sagen, es herrscht (im Gegensatz zur Verwendung des PRESENT PERFECT) eine DISTANZ zum Geschehen. Meistens wird – und auch das kann eine Abgrenzung zu PRESENT PERFECT sein – ein Zeitpunkt des Geschehens genannt.

I saw her a second ago.
Last year we spent Christmas at a chalet in the Swiss Alps.
Let me tell you what happened: When I did my shopping, a man collapsed in the supermarket.
When I was little, I had curly hair.

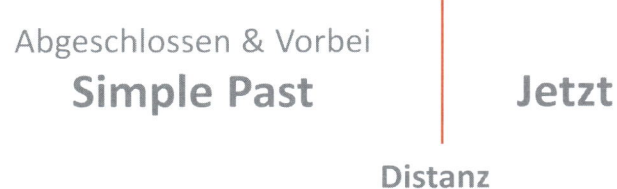

Abgeschlossen & Vorbei

Simple Past | Jetzt

Distanz

> **!** Die häufigsten Fehler bei der Verwendung des SIMPLE PAST sind die Verwendung der richtigen Form des Verbs = 2. FORM und die richtige Verwendung des Hilfsverbs to do bei FRAGE und VERNEINUNG, hier in der Form von did/didn't.

Typische Signalwörter sind Zeitpunkte in der Vergangenheit:
yesterday, last week, in 1995, a minute ago

Simple Past bilden

Aussage

Das SIMPLE PAST ist die 2. FORM des Verbs. Sie ist für diese Zeit reserviert und gilt für alle Personen I, you, he, she, it, we, you, they. Regelmäßige Verben erhalten die Endung -ed, unmäßige Verben haben eigene Formen, die man lernen muss, siehe Liste auf S. 75.

1. FORM = INFINITIV	2. FORM = SIMPLE PAST	3. FORM = PARTIZIP PERFEKT
to build	built	built
to go	went	gone
to drive	drove	driven
to speak	spoke	spoken
to see	saw	seen

I	built	a house.
You	dreamt	of building a house.
He	bought	a house.
She	moved	in soon afterwards.
It	was	a very nice house.
We	visited	them in September.
You	came	to the party.
They	were	very happy there.

Verneinung

Die Verneinung wird wie beim SIMPLE PRESENT mit dem Hilfsverb do gebildet, aber in seiner 2. FORM = did + not/didn't in Verbindung mit dem INFINITIV.

		INFINITIV	
I	did not/didn't	get	a present.
You	did not/didn't	buy	me one. Why?
He	did not/didn't	do	it on purpose.
She	did not/didn't	find	it very amusing.
It	did not/didn't	say	so on the invitation.
We	did not/didn't	think	about it, really.
You	did not/didn't	bring	one either, DID you?
They	did not/didn't	invite	them ever again!

Frage

Auch die Frage wird mit did und in Verbindung mit dem INFINITIV des Hauptverbs gebildet. Did rückt dann an den SATZANFANG, Fragewörter stehen noch vor dem did.

		INFINITIV	
Did	I	tell	you?
Did	you	do	that?
Did	he	send	you the parcel?
Did	she	say	he would?
Did	it	work	out for you?
Where did	we	meet	last week?
Did	you	go	to Spain in the end?
Did	they	have	a party last week?

> ❗ AUSNAHME: Bei der Verwendung des Fragewortes who kommt der Satz ohne did aus:
>
> | Who | came | home late? |
> |---|---|---|
> | Who | won | the race? |

> ❗ HINWEIS: Did und die 2. FORM des Verbs gehören nie zusammen in einen Satz! Einmal Vergangenheit reicht. Did she liked the film? ist *falsch*!

Unregelmäßige Verben (Auszug)

Es hilft leider nichts, die 2. und 3. FORM der unregelmäßigen Verben muss man auswendig lernen. Hier zur Wiederholung eine Liste der gebräuchlichsten Verben mit der jeweils gängigsten Bedeutung.

1. FORM	2. FORM	3. FORM	
to be	was/were	been	sein
to become	became	become	werden
to begin	began	begun	beginnen
to bite	bit	bitten	beißen
to bring	brought	brought	bringen
to break	broke	broken	(zer)brechen
to build	built	built	bauen
to buy	bought	bought	kaufen
to catch	caught	caught	fangen
to come	came	come	kommen
to do	did	done	tun, machen
to drink	drank	drunk	trinken
to drive	drove	driven	fahren
to eat	ate	eaten	essen
to fall	fell	fallen	fallen
to feel	felt	felt	fühlen
to find	found	found	finden
to fly	flew	flown	fliegen
to forget	forgot	forgotten	vergessen
to get	got	got	bekommen
to give	gave	given	geben
to go	went	gone	gehen
to have	had	had	haben
to hear	heard	heard	hören
to hide	hid	hidden	verstecken
to hit	hit	hit	schlagen

to hold	held	held	halten
to hurt	hurt	hurt	verletzen
to keep	kept	kept	behalten
to know	knew	known	wissen
to lay	laid	laid	legen
to lead	led	led	(an)führen
to lend	lent	lent	leihen
to let	let	let	(zu)lassen
to lie	lay	lain	liegen
to light	lit	lit	anzünden
to lose	lost	lost	verlieren
to make	made	made	machen
to mean	meant	meant	bedeuten
to meet	met	met	treffen
to pay	paid	paid	bezahlen
to put	put	put	(hin)stellen
to read	read	read	lesen
to ride	rode	ridden	reiten
to ring	rang	rung	anrufen
to run	ran	run	laufen
to say	said	said	sagen
to see	saw	seen	sehen
to sell	sold	sold	verkaufen
to send	sent	sent	senden
to shake	shook	shaken	schütteln
to shoot	shot	shot	schießen
to sing	sang	sung	singen
to sit	sat	sat	sitzen
to speak	spoke	spoken	sprechen
to spend	spent	spent	ausgeben
to stand	stood	stood	stehen
to swim	swam	swum	schwimmen
to take	took	taken	nehmen

to teach	taught	taught	unterrichten
to tell	told	told	erzählen
to think	thought	thought	denken
to throw	threw	thrown	werfen
to understand	understood	understood	verstehen
to wake	woke	woken	wecken
to wear	wore	worn	tragen
to win	won	won	gewinnen
to write	wrote	written	schreiben

To be = was/were

Be gehört zu den unregelmäßigen Verben und wie schon beim SIMPLE PRESENT (S. 35) bildet auch beim SIMPLE PAST be eine Ausnahme und kommt bei VERNEINUNG und FRAGE ohne did aus.

to be in der 2. FORM = was/were

1. FORM	2. FORM	3. FORM
to be	was/were	been
was	für	I, he, she, it
were	für	you, we, they

Achtung: Im Prinzip steht were für die Plural-Personen (we, you, they), wird aber auch für das Singular-you verwendet!

> Where were you? (Mother asks son.)
> I looked for you, but you weren't there!

Simple Past bilden mit be

AUSSAGE	VERNEINUNG	FRAGE
I was there.	I was not/wasn't.	Was I really?

You were very nice.	You were not/weren't nice.	Were you nice?
He/she was angry.	It was not/wasn't very fair.	Was it fair?
We were young.	We were not/weren't young.	Were we young?
You were 12 people.	You were not/weren't many.	Were you many?
They were children.	They were not/weren't happy.	Were they?

To do = did

Do kann gleichzeitig als Vollverb UND Hilfsverb im selben Satz vorkommen:

	HILFSVERB	VOLLVERB		
You	-----		did	your homework.	Aussage
I	didn't		do	my homework yesterday.	Verneinung
	Did	I	do	my homework?	Frage
It	------		did	her a lot of good.	Aussage
He	didn't		do	the washing up this morning.	Verneinung
How	did	she	do	that?	Frage
It	------		did	me a lot of good.	Aussage
We	didn't		do	anything today.	Verneinung
	Did	they	do	nothing all day?	Frage

Must = have to

Das SIMPLE PAST von must stellt Lernende regelmäßig vor Schwie-
rigkeiten, denn es existiert weder eine 2. noch eine 3. FORM (siehe
Modalverben, S. 176). Aber Modalverben haben ERSATZFORMEN.
Für must ist es have to und diese wird für die Vergangenheit benutzt.
In Sätzen der GEGENWART sind must und have to austauschbar:

| We must go to school today. | oder | We have to go to school today. |
| They must take care. | oder | They have to take care. |

Must

1. FORM	2. FORM	3. FORM
to have (to)	had (to)	had (to)

Simple Past bilden mit must

AUSSAGE	VERNEINUNG	FRAGE
I must be on time.	I didn't have to be on time.	Did I have to …?
You must be quick.	You didn't have to be quick.	Did you have to …?
She must get up.	She didn't have to get up.	Did she have to …?
We must be quiet.	We didn't have to be quiet.	Did we have to …?
They must lie.	They didn't have to lie.	Did they have to …?

Simple Past und Simple Present – Parallelen

Hier möchte ich auf die Logik der englischen Grammatik hinweisen. In der Gegenwartsform SIMPLE PRESENT muss bei der FRAGE + VERNEINUNG to do als Hilfsverb verwendet werden. Genauso ist es in der Vergangenheitsform SIMPLE PAST, dann aber to do in der Vergangenheitsform did. Merkt man sich das einmal richtig, fällt es leichter, zwischen den Zeiten die Parallelen zu sehen und im richtigen Moment korrekt anzuwenden.

PRESENT	PAST	
do + INFINITIV	did + INFINITIV	= Frage
do/does not + INFINITIV	did not + INFINITIV	= Verneinung

Simple Past in a nutshell

SIMPLE PAST = 2. FORM
FRAGE + VERNEINUNG mit did + INFINITIV
Häufig wird ein Zeitpunkt genannt
Geschehen vorbei, wir erzählen, berichten
aus der Distanz

Fragen, Unklarheiten, Notizen

Für die Sportfans –
SIMPLE PAST in ATHLETICS-NEWS
"The sportswear giants (Adidas) allegedly made the decision to step away from world athletics' governing body and their 11-year contract earlier this week."

www.mirror.co.uk/sport/other-sports/athletics

Beispielsätze Simple Past

When I was little, I lived abroad, in Hungary.
I grew up with two sisters and three brothers.
Last year the company had a turnover of over 34bn Euros.
Mother went shopping this morning and still hasn't come back.
Why did they not buy the other car? I thought it looked much better.
We all spent two weeks in Spain and the holiday was a real success.
My great-grand-father died during the war.
Did you think of taking the present?
Where was it? I put it on the table this morning.
Don't tell me you didn't take it with you?
The film was good. I remember we laughed very much.
We went to Spain last summer.
I didn't get the money from the bank.
He confessed his love to her.
He introduced me to his parents.
To whom did you show the letter?
It was a compliment for me.
We didn't live in a house when I was little.
Did you get the invitation I posted to you?

Redewendungen Simple Past

We got carried away by the
  idea of winning the lottery.   Wir ließen uns mitreißen
After all that physical work
  I was out for the count.   Ich habe tief und fest geschlafen

Praxis

It's your turn
Übung 12
Sätze bilden

a. Wann fand das letzte Meeting statt?

_____

b. Habt ihr letzten Sommer nicht auf den Malediven verbracht?

_____

c. Ich war neunzehn, als ich mit der Schule fertig war.

_____

d. Freunde von uns sind Anfang des Jahres in die USA gezogen.

_____

e. Vor zwei Wochen haben wir unser neues Auto bestellt.

_____

f. Das Haus fiel beim letzten Sturm zusammen.

_____

g. Sarah hat sich gestern entschieden, das Haus zu verkaufen.

_____

h. Wir haben unsere Eltern letzte Woche besucht.

_____

i. Vor einer Minute war sie hier.

_____

j. Früher verging die Zeit schneller.

_____

Übung 13
Richtige Verbform einsetzen – SIMPLE PAST

a. This school (to exist) _____ 200 years ago. Many

famous people (to be) _____ students here. There

(to be) _____ many rich merchants who (to support)

_____ _____ the school. Usually it (to get)

_____ donations of more than 400,000 Pounds a year.

b. (you, to think) _____ she (to come) _____

home earlier than that?

c. I (not to be) _____ surprised that they (to win)

_____ the lottery. They always win.

d. When it (to get) _____ dark outside, they (to take)

_____ their belongings and (to sneak) _____

out of the back door. They (not to catch) _____

them escaping, so they (to be) _____ very relieved.

e. When we (to be) _____ little, we (must) _____

behave very nicely. We (not to be) _____ allowed to

speak when adults were talking. Neither (to be) _____

we allowed to watch TV at night. I (to find) _____ it

(not to harm) _____ me or my sister.

f. What (you, to do) _____ during your holiday? – Most of

the time we (to chill) _____ at the pool. But some days

we (to go on) _____ excursions into the woods.

g. (you, to know) _____ Mr. Smith, the math prof at

university? No, he (not to be) _____ there when I

(to be) _____.

h. I bet she (not to say) _____ anything to him at all!

Simple Past oder Present Perfect?

Am Beispiel soll noch einmal der Unterschied zwischen SIMPLE PAST und PRESENT PERFECT verdeutlicht werden. Wir rufen in Erinnerung: beim PRESENT PERFECT besteht ein direkter, gefühlter Bezug zum JETZT.

Nehmen wir diesen Satz: *Wo warst du?*

SIMPLE PAST: Where were you (when I needed you most)?

PRESENT PERFECT: Where have you been? (Sohn kommt heim, die Mutter fragt.)

Wie dieser Satz im Englischen lauten muss, hängt ganz von dem Zusammenhang ab. Im ersten Fall wird durch den Zusatz deutlich, dass von einem Zeitpunkt die Rede ist, der eindeutig in der Vergangenheit liegt: Er brauchte jemanden *damals*, heute nicht mehr. Im zweiten

Fall besteht ein direkter Bezug zum Moment des Sprechens JETZT: Die Mutter hatte sich gerade gewundert, wo ihr Sohn war.

Ergo: In der Regel kann man durch den Zusammenhang sehr genau sagen, wann SIMPLE PAST verwendet werden muss, spätestens wenn eindeutige Zeitangaben gefallen sind wie yesterday, last year, sometime ago.

Simple Past
Abgeschlossen

oder

Present Perfect
Bezug zur Gegenwart

Eine der Tücken beim Sprachen-Lernen ist, dass wir dazu tendieren, wörtlich zu übersetzen, wovon man sich lösen muss. Der Satz *Wir haben meine Eltern letzte Woche besucht* würde unter Umständen übersetzt mit We have visited my parents last week. Richtig wäre hier aber: We visited my parents last week. Es wird eindeutig über etwas berichtet, das einmalig in der Vergangenheit passiert ist = SIMPLE PAST. Die Entscheidung, ob wir SIMPLE PAST oder PRESENT PERFECT verwenden sollen, hängt im Englischen einzig und allein davon ab, ob ein BEZUG zur GEGENWART besteht oder nicht. Noch ein Beispiel aus dem Sport – im ersten Beispiel sind Hinweise auf den Zeitpunkt des Geschehens hervorgehoben.

Simple Past

Watson lost the first set 6-1 and asked for the match to be stopped at just after 21:00 BST (British Summer Time) after taking the second set 6-3 on Monday night. The same night, Naomi Broady lost 7-6 (7-5) 6-3 to Colombia's Mariana Duque-Marino. The British number three was unable to match the success of her younger brother Liam, who won his first-round match earlier in the day.

(BBC NEWS, 29 June 15)

Present Perfect

Manchester United defender Phil Jones has signed a new contract that will keep him at the club until June 2019. The 23-year-old England international has made 128 appearances for United but has struggled with injuries during his four years at the club.

(BBC NES, 29 June 15)

Praxis

It's your Turn
Übung 14

SIMPLE PAST oder PRESENT PERFECT?

a. Dein Paket ist angekommen.

_____

b. Hast du meinen Kugelschreiber gesehen?

_____

c. Unser Nachbar hatte vor drei Monaten einen Unfall.

_____

d. Sie hat den Vertrag am Ende der letzten Saison unterzeichnet.

_____

e. Dein Paket ist heute Morgen angekommen.

_____

f. Peter kannte viele Gedichte auswendig.

_____

g. Charles Dickens lebte im 19. Jahrhundert.

_____

h. Eine große Welle hat das Schiff in zwei Teile zerbrochen. (News)

_____

i. Wie lange liest du schon an dem Buch?

_____

j. Er ist ausgewählt worden.

_____

Übung 15

SIMPLE PRESENT oder PRESENT PERFECT CONTINUOUS

a. Er geht jede Woche einmal zum Tennis.

He (to play) _____ tennis once a week.

b. Seit zwei Jahren fährt sie mit dem Auto zur Arbeit.

She (to drive) _____ to work by car for two

years.

c. Sie gehen sehr oft ins Kino.

They (to go) _____ to the cinema very often.

d. Er lebt seit 2012 in Spanien.

He (to live) _____ in Spain since 1995.

e. Sie übt jeden Tag Klavier.

   She (to practice) _____ the piano every day.

f. Ich warte den ganzen Morgen auf ein Paket.

   I (to wait) _____ for a parcel all morning.

Übung 16
PRESENT PERFECT CONTINUOUS bilden

a. Seit der Landung warten die Passagiere auf den Bus.

   _____

b. Wohnt ihr schon lange in diesem Haus?

   _____

c. Du bastelst seit einer Ewigkeit an dem Auto herum!

   _____

d. Wir gehen seit Jahren zu Doktor Scott.

   _____

e. Die Klasse schreibt seit einer Stunde einen Test.

   _____

f. Der Lärm hält seit Stunden an.

   _____

g. Sie spielen seit heute Morgen in ihrem Zimmer.

   _____

h. Die Gerüchte halten sich seit Monaten.

   _____

Past Perfect

= Vorvergangenheit
Wird verwendet
1. bei zwei aufeinanderfolgenden Handlungen in der Vergangenheit,
2. für die Handlung, die ZUERST stattfand.

PAST PERFECT ist die VORVERGANGENHEIT und muss immer dann verwendet werden, wenn der Sprecher bereits in der Vergangenheit erzählt, dann aber zeitlich EINE STUFE ZURÜCKGEHT. Die vom Sprecher aus weiter zurückliegende Zeit steht im PAST PERFECT. Achtung: PAST PERFECT taucht meistens in einem eigenen Satzteil auf, im anderen Satzteil steht dann oft SIMPLE PAST. Es wird auch verwendet, wenn über etwas gesprochen wird, dass bis zu einem Zeitpunkt in der Vergangenheit, zeitlich also davor, passiert ist.

ZEITLICH	ZEITLICH
2 STUFEN ZURÜCK	1 STUFE ZURÜCK
PAST PERFECT	SIMPLE PAST

She came home at 11 am.

Her son had left earlier.

PAST PERFECT wird mit dem Partizip Perfekt = 3. FORM und der VERGANGENHEITSFORM von to have = had gebildet.

> **!** Diese Zeit ist Ungeübten meistens nicht (mehr) geläufig und wird daher von ihnen selten verwendet.

Signalwörter (Beispiele)
already, before, as soon as, after

Aussage

	SATZTEIL I	SATZTEIL II
I	had seen the thief	just before he broke in.
You	had left the house	before they came home.
She	had noticed the car	a second before it hit her.
He	had found the key	just before he came in.
We	had met at school	long before we moved in together.
They	had known each other for 20 years	before they got married.

Es gibt also zwei Satzteile.

 Welcher Teil vorne steht, ist dabei egal!

Der Sinn bleibt dabei derselbe, auch wenn man die Satzteile ver-
tauscht:

I had seen the thief just before he broke in.

Just before he broke in, I had seen the thief.

Beispiele:

She had watched a horror movie before she went to bed.

She didn't sleep as well as she had thought she would.

After Amy had gone home it started to rain.

She got wet because she hadn't thought of bringing an umbrella.

When they arrived the game had already started.

Abkürzungen

Auch beim PAST PERFECT gibt es Kurzformen:

I had seen the thief … wird zu I'd seen the thief …

Bei den Abkürzungen muss man schon genau hinhören, denn sowohl I've had (PRESENT PERFECT) als auch I'd had (PAST PERFECT) kann man so schnell aussprechen, dass es verschluckt wird.

I'd seen the thief …
You'd left the house …
She'd noticed the car …
He'd found the key …
We'd met at school …
They'd known each other for 20 years …

Verneinung

Bei der Verneinung wird ein not eingefügt:

I had not/hadn't left the house before they came home.

She had not/hadn't found the key before he returned.

They had not/hadn't seen each other for years and yet got married.

Frage

Hier wird das had an den Satzanfang gestellt.

Had you left in time before they closed?

Had he found a publisher before he finished writing?

Why had you kept the papers though you knew you wouldn't need them anymore?

Aus der Praxis: PAST PERFECT kommt im Sprachgebrauch sicher nicht ganz so häufig vor wie beispielsweise PRESENT PERFECT, SIMPLE PAST, PRESENT oder die Zukunftsformen. Dennoch wird man beim Hören und/oder Lesen damit in Berührung kommen und dann ist es wichtig zu wissen, was mit diesen Sätzen ausgedrückt wird.

To have

Wie bei PRESENT PERFECT kann auch bei PAST PERFECT to have
als Vollverb *und* als Hilfsverb innerhalb eines Satzes vorkommen:
He was very tired because he <u>had had</u> an extremely hard week at work.
He <u>had had</u> an extremely hard week at work, so he was very tired.

Past Perfect und Present Perfect – Parallelen

Hier wieder ein Verweis auf die Logik der englischen Grammatik. In
der Gegenwartsform PRESENT PERFECT werden bei der Frage +
Verneinung have/has + 3. FORM des Verbs verwendet. In der Vergangenheitsform PAST PERFECT wird daraus had + 3. Form des
Verbs.

PRESENT | PAST
have/has + 3. FORM   had + 3. FORM   = Aussage + Frage
have/has not + 3. FORM   had not + 3. FORM = Verneinung

Past Perfect Continuous

= Verlaufsform des PAST PERFECT
Auch PAST PERFECT hat eine Verlaufsform = CONTINUOUS. Wie
alle CONTINUOUS-Zeiten verweist sie auf eine Zeitspanne.

ZEITLICH   ZEITLICH
2 STUFEN ZURÜCK   1 STUFE ZURÜCK
PAST PERFECT CONTINUOUS   SIMPLE PAST

She came home at 11 am.

Her son had been waiting for her

Zeitspanne

Hier wird betont, dass ihr Sohn schon *die ganze Zeit* gewartet hatte!

PAST PERFECT CONTINUOUS bilden
had + been + ing

Aussage

I had <u>been</u> waiting a really long time before you finally came!
She had <u>been</u> watching TV all afternoon, so she was really tired.
They had <u>been</u> hoping that she would recover.

Verneinung

You had not/hadn't <u>been</u> walking long before you got there, had you?
He had not/hadn't <u>been</u> missing her at all during the weekend.
They had not/hadn't <u>been</u> waiting a long time before you came home.

Frage

Bei der Bildung von Fragen, die einen längeren Zeitraum in der Vergangenheit betreffen (CONTINUOUS), kommt das had an den Satzanfang:
Had he <u>been</u> living on his own before he got married?
Had he <u>been</u> dating mum, before she met dad?
Had they <u>been</u> waiting long before you got there?

! Für Anfänger sind die anderen Zeiten wichtiger als diese, denn sie wird seltener verwendet und führt leicht zu Verunsicherungen.

Tipp: PAST PERFECT CONTINUOUS erst anschauen, wenn die anderen Zeiten sicher in der Anwendung sind.

Past Perfect in a nutshell

had + **3. FORM**
VORVERGANGENHEIT
Verlaufsform had + been + ing
zwei Satzteile

Fragen, Unklarheiten, Notizen

Für die Sportfans –
PAST PERFECT in TENNIS-NEWS
"Murray had never dropped a set to Tomic in the pair's three previous meetings but a question mark surrounded his focus after the unnerving events over the weekend."
  www.telegraph.co.uk/sport/tennis/andymurray

Beispielsätze Past Perfect
They had arrived late, so there was no food left.
They had done everything required – and still didn't get the job.
He had had accidents before this last one.
When we came home, the neighbour had left a message.
We thought no one was at home, because the curtains hadn't been opened all day.

Praxis

It's your turn
Übung 17
SÄTZE BILDEN mit PAST PERFECT

a. They (to spend) _____ their honeymoon in Paris

where they (to meet) _____ two years before.

b. When Alice (to do) _____ the shopping, she (to pick

up) _____ her children from school.

c. He (to show) _____ us the place where he (to hurt)

_____ his leg.

d. I (to look) _____ at the photos that he (to send)

_____

e. Yesterday I (to read) _____ an interesting article

which my teacher (to recommend) _____ to me.

f. I (not to touch) _____ a snake before that day.

g. Andy (to win) _____ the match although he (not to

play) _____ squash before.

h. When I (to leave) _____ the house, I (not to have)

_____ breakfast.

Übung 18
PRESENT PERFECT oder PAST PERFECT

a. Wir sind gerade erst angekommen.

_____

b. Wir waren gerade erst losgefahren.

_____

c. Ich hatte ihn vorher schon mal gesehen.

_____

d. Seid ihr schon fertig mit dem Staubsaugen?

_____

e. Ich habe genug davon!

_____

f. Ich hatte einfach genug.

_____

g. Das hatte ich vorher noch nicht gesehen.

_____

h. Wir haben uns gestritten.

_____

Übung 19
SIMPLE PAST oder PAST PERFECT

a. Last year we (to build) _____ our house,

b. after we (to get) _____ the land.

c. We (to leave) _____ the car at the garage before

d. we (to catch) _____ the bus home.

e. Be honest, you (not to think) _____ about the size

f. before you (to start) _____ building it.

g. He (to catch) _____ the fish. Before that

h. he (already, to put) _____ the fire on.

Übung 20
SÄTZE BILDEN im PAST PERFECT

a. I (not to touch) _____ an elephant before.

b. When I left the house, she (not to have) _____

   breakfast yet.

c. I looked at the paper she (to give) _____ me.

d. He showed us the place where he (to have) _____

   the accident.

e. (he, to speak) _____ to you before he called us?

Past Continuous

= Verlaufsform der Vergangenheit

Wird verwendet

1. bei zwei gleichzeitigen Handlungen in der Vergangenheit,
2. wenn eine Handlung in der Vergangenheit über einen längeren Zeitraum andauert.

PAST CONTINUOUS (= PAST PROGRESSIVE) ist die VERLAUFS-FORM der Vergangenheit. Sie hat zwei Funktionen: Zum einen drückt sie aus, dass in der Vergangenheit etwas *um einen bestimmten Zeitpunkt herum* geschah. Zum anderen benötigen wir sie, wenn mehrere Handlungen in der Vergangenheit *gleichzeitig* passieren. Diejenige, die länger andauert, quasi eine Hintergrundhandlung, steht dabei im PAST CONTINUOUS, die zweite Handlung im SIMPLE PAST. Hier wird in der Regel dann when (als) benutzt.

Beispiel:

Als ich nach Hause kam, spielten meine Brüder Fußball im Garten.

When I came home, my brothers were playing football in the garden.

My brothers were playing football in the garden when I came home.

Welcher der zwei Satzteile vorne steht, ist egal.

Wichtig ist hier: Die Brüder spielten Fußball *bevor, während und nachdem* ich nach Hause kam.

Zum Vergleich: When I came home, my brothers played football in the garden.

Hier werden zwei Handlungen aufgezählt, was bedeutet: Die Brüder begannen mit dem Fußballspielen erst, *als ich nach Hause kam*!

PAST CONTINUOUS

Zeitspanne

The boys were playing.

SIMPLE PAST

X

Punktuell

She came home.

Signalwörter (Beispiele)
while, when, but, before

> ! Das PAST CONTINUOUS ist bei den meisten Ungeübten etwas verstaubt. Es wurde gelernt, wird aber nicht unbedingt angewendet, die Bildung macht dabei weniger Schwierigkeiten.

HINWEIS: Wir können mit dem PAST CONTINUOUS lebendig wiedergeben, was wir *um einen bestimmten Zeitpunkt herum* in der Vergangenheit gemacht haben, also die Tätigkeit betonen.
Beispiel: Was hast du gestern Abend um 20 Uhr gemacht?
I was watching the news.

Oder über eine Reise berichten:
When I was in the States last month, I was driving around all the time, my friends and I were meeting in pubs, at the beach and we were going to a lot of concerts.
This Christmas, I spent with my family and we were all having a wonderful time together. The children were playing very nicely together and the men were getting on very well most of the time, which was nice.

Past Continuous bilden

Aussage

CONTINUOUS hat immer eine ing-Endung, hier braucht es die Vergangenheit = 2. FORM von to be = was/were vor dem Verb mit -ing.
was/were + looking

Die Reihenfolge der Satzteile ist dabei egal:
I was cutting the tree, when it started to rain.
When it started to rain, I was cutting the tree.

Weitere Beispiele:
You were watching your favourite programme but mom turned it off.
He was thinking of buying a car but he suddenly lost his job.
It was snowing big flakes when the children built a snowman.
We were spending some time abroad when a lightning struck our house.
They were climbing the hill, when the weather changed.

Verneinung

Auch hier wird das not eingefügt.
I was not/wasn't hiking much when I was in Australia.
You were not/weren't looking very happy when you got the price.
She was not/wasn't telling the truth all the time.
They were not/weren't listening to what the teacher said.

Frage

Was/were werden an den Satzanfang gestellt.

Was I sleeping when you came in?

When I passed by at the café weren't you having tea with Laura?

Was it raining heavily during your walk?

Were we living with Aunt Susan when I was little?

Past Continuous und Present Continuous – Parallelen

Hier wieder ein Verweis auf die Logik, der die englische Grammatik folgt. In der Gegenwartsform PRESENT CONTINUOUS wird die entsprechende Form von to be verwendet am/is/are + ing. In der Vergangenheitsform PAST CONTINUOUS wird entsprechend was/were + ing verwendet.

PRESENT	PAST	
am/is/are + ing	was/were + ing	= Aussage + Frage
am/is/are not + ing	was/were not + ing	= Verneinung

Past Continuous in a nutshell

was/were + ing

Verlaufsform in der Vergangenheit

zwei Handlungen GLEICHZEITIG,

Hintergrundhandlung

zwei Satzteile

Fragen, Unklarheiten, Notizen

Für Die Sportfans –

PAST CONTINUOUS in (HORSE) RACING-NEWS

"Ruby Walsh (horse name) was chasing his fourth win of an impressive opening day but the clear 4/7 favourite fell after throwing herself at the final hurdle."

  www.mirror.co.uk/sport/horse-racing

Beispielsätze Past Continuous

When he called they were having breakfast.
Were you sleeping? I am sorry I woke you up!
We were having a good time during our holidays.
At the wedding, the parents were meeting their friends for the first time.
During the exam I believe you weren't trying hard enough!
She was painting the chairs when the storm started.
He was taking the children to school when the accident happened.
We were begging for more, but she didn't give in.
Were you keeping it a secret all the time?
We were trying to get into university all year.

Praxis

It's your turn
Übung 21
SÄTZE BILDEN im PAST CONTINUOUS

a. as soon as/sun out/the snowman/melt

_____

b. during their excursion/they/explore/new territories

_____

c. on the phone/the secretary/print out/a document

_____

d. the girls/not/concentrate/on the task

_____

e. mother/come home/David/not/practice/the piano

_____

f. during/show/Jill/dance

_____

g. your cousins/swim/in the lake/start to rain

_____

h. during visit/the professor/answer/questions of/the student

_____

Zukunft

Durch welche Zeiten wird Zukunft ausgedrückt?

Um auszudrücken, dass etwas in der Zukunft geschieht, gibt es im Englischen verschiedene Möglichkeiten. Das WILL FUTURE steht dabei ganz vorne, es ist am geläufigsten. Das PRESENT CONTINUOUS, das zeigt die Praxis, ist selten als Form der Zukunft bekannt, dennoch wird es im Sprachgebrauch häufig verwendet, mindestens ebenso häufig wie das GOING-TO FUTURE.

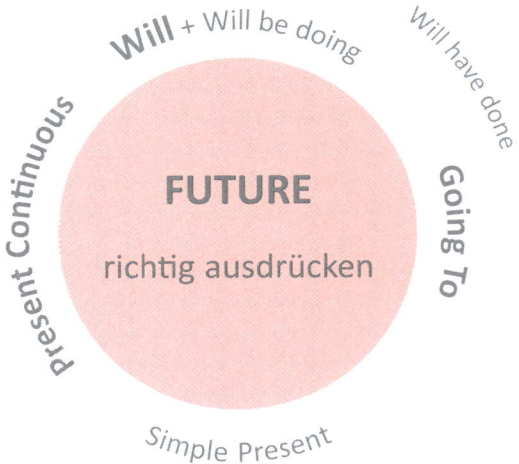

WILL	I'm sure it will rain tomorrow.
GOING TO	We are going to buy a new car next spring.
PRESENT CONTINUOUS	Are we meeting tonight at 20 hours then?
SIMPLE PRESENT	The park closes at 7:30 pm.
WILL BE DOING	I will be studying next year this time.
WILL HAVE DONE	By the time we get there she will have called.

Bei der Entscheidung für die jeweils richtige Zeitform geht es vor allem darum, wie sicher es ist, dass etwas eintrifft, wie weit die Planung vorangeschritten ist und wie weit in der Zukunft noch liegt, was passieren wird. Nachstehend werden die Kriterien für jede Form im Einzelnen aufgeführt.

Will Future

Will wird verwendet, wenn etwas spontan geäußert wird, oder bei Vorhersagen und Vermutungen, die der Sprecher nicht beeinflussen kann. Spontane Äußerungen sind solche, die einem Sprecher im Moment einfallen oder sich aus einer Situation ergeben. Ebenfalls werden Angebote damit ausgesprochen und Versprechen. Und ebenso, dass wir „wollen" meinen bzw. „bereit sein".

Spontan
Will you come to the cinema with us tonight?
I will just pop downstairs to get some lunch.
The phone is ringing. Sarah: I will get it.

Vorhersagen
It will rain this afternoon. – It said so on the news and the sky is dark.
It will not be enough to do nothing for the exam.
I think Germany will win the European Championship.

Angebote, Versprechen
We'll send you an email.
I'll see you tomorrow.
Susan will be at the meeting.

„wollen" meinen, „bereit sein"

I hope they will come to our wedding.
I am sure Sue will come with us if we ask her.
Stephen says he will help us with the move.

> **!** Ist man unsicher bei der Verwendung der korrekten Zeitform für die Zukunft, besteht immer die Option, das WILL FUTURE zu verwenden. Es wird auf jeden Fall verstanden. Für gutes Englisch sollte man allerdings auch wissen, warum es die weiteren Zukunftsformen gibt, und sie anwenden können.

Will Future bilden

Aussage

Das WILL FUTURE besteht immer aus will und dem INFINITIV = GRUNDFORM des Verbs.

Will +

Infinitiv

	will	+ INFINITIV	
I	will	get	it. Telefon klingelt
You	will	lose	the purse in this pocket.
He	will	stay	at home, he has just decided.
She	will	drop in	tonight to fetch the medicine, ok?
It	will	get	a mouse and bring it to me.
We	will	wait	and see.
You	will	meet	him this afternoon.
They	will	eat	later.

Abkürzungen

In der gesprochenen Sprache werden meistens Abkürzungen verwendet. Will wird zu 'll. Manchmal muss man genau hinhören.

I'll see.	You'll see.	He'll see.	She'll see.
It'll see.	We'll see.	You'll see.	They'll see.

Verneinung + not = won't

Will not wird abgekürzt zu won't. Man kann die eine oder die andere Form verwenden. will not betont die Verneinung etwas stärker.

FRAGE – will kommt an den SATZANFANG			VERNEINUNG
Will	I	get good marks?	No, you won't.
Will	you	get some lunch for us?	No, I will not.
Will	he	come home soon?	No, he won't.
Will	she	bring her watch?	No, she will not.
Will	it	end soon enough?	No, it won't.
Will	we	find somewhere new?	No, we will not.
Will	you	stay the night?	No, we won't.
Will	they	sign the contract?	No, they will not.

> **!** Eine Fehlerquelle ist die Unterscheidung von will und want. Grundsätzlich darf will (werden) nicht mit want (wollen, möchten, ein Wunsch) verwechselt werden! Aber: Wie oben erwähnt, wird will auch verwendet, wenn „bereit sein/wollen" gemeint ist. Ein kleiner Unterschied ist erkennbar: Verwendet der Sprecher want, steht der Wunsch im Fokus, bei will dagegen eher der Plan.

Was willst, möchtest du dagegen tun?

What do you want to do about it?	Frage nach dem Wunsch
What will you do about it?	Frage nach dem Plan

Wirst du bleiben?
Do you want to stay?   Frage nach dem Wunsch
Will you stay?   Frage nach dem Plan

Will Future in a nutshell

will + INFINITIV

SPONTAN, VERMUTUNG, VORHERSAGEN,
ANGEBOT, VERSPRECHEN

Fragen, Unklarheiten, Notizen

Für die Sportfans –

WILL FUTURE in RUGBY-NEWS

"However, the 12 Premiership clubs will see their capital rise to £6.5m per club for 2016-17 and £7m for 2017-18."

   www.bbc.com/sport/rugby-union

Beispielsätze Will Future

I am sure you will need a coat later this evening.

Will you please stop crying!

I can't say what he will do after he has found a job.

We've just decided: We'll have a barbecue tonight.

Don't forget to buy milk! – No, I won't.

I'll call it a day.   Feierabend machen

I will put my best foot forward.   sein Bestes geben

Will be doing Future (Future Continuous)

= Verlaufsform

Das WILL BE DOING FUTURE drückt aus, dass zu einem Zeitpunkt in der Zukunft etwas über einen längeren Zeitraum geschieht. Zum Beispiel:

Wenn du nach Hause kommst, wird Max gerade Klavier üben, sei also bitte leise.

When you get home, Max will be practicing the piano, so please be quiet.

Weitere Beispiele:

This time next year, I will be studying at Bristol University.

Next Monday, you will be flying home.

Das FUTURE CONTINUOUS wird ebenfalls verwendet, wenn wir *annehmen*, dass gerade etwas passiert.

Don't phone grandma now, she'll be having dinner.

You will be getting into trouble, if you carry on behaving like this.

Hinweis: Diese Zeit wird nicht allzu häufig gebraucht, denn sie beschreibt eine spezielle Handlung in der Zukunft, etwas über das wir in der Regel nicht allzu oft reden. Aber: Diese Zeit zu kennen und anwenden zu können, das ist gutes Englisch.

Will be doing Future bilden

Die Bildung ist bei allen Personen gleich: will + be + ing
Bei der Verneinung wird won't benutzt.

FRAGE   Will she be doing the washing up today?
VERNEINUNG   No, she won't be doing it today, she did it yesterday.
AUSSAGE   You will be doing it instead!

Für die Sportfans –
WILL BE DOING FUTURE in RALLYE-NEWS
"The WRC (World Rally Championship) returns to Europe for Rally Portugal where Elfyn Evans will be hoping to impress in the WRC2."
    www.bbc.co.uk/programmes

Beispielsätze will be doing Future
If you go there you will be doing me a great favour.
They'll be missing their mother if she really leaves.
I will be watching football when you get home.
At 7 pm tomorrow I will be working in the pub.
When you come to America, I will still be studying here.
They will be doing five laps on the run.

Will have done Future (Future Perfect)

Diese Zeit brauchen wir, wenn wir sagen wollen: Zu einem Zeitpunkt in der Zukunft wird etwas Bestimmtes passiert sein, also in der *Zwischenzeit* zwischen JETZT und DANN.

Beispiel:

Mama kommt um acht heute Abend nach Hause. Ich hoffe, du hast bis dahin deine Hausaufgaben fertig.

Mom is coming home at 8 pm tonight. I hope you will <u>have</u> finished your homework by then.

Weitere Beispiele:

Next year they will <u>have</u> been married for 17 years.

Damn, we are late. The film will <u>have</u> started by the time we get there.

Will have done Future bilden

Die Bildung ist bei allen Personen gleich: will + have + 3. FORM
Bei der Verneinung wird won't benutzt.

FRAGE	Will she <u>have</u> got up by then?
VERNEINUNG	No, she won't <u>have</u> seen me before the wedding.
AUSSAGE	You will <u>have</u> collected the books before we meet.

> **!** Das WILL HAVE DONE FUTURE (FUTURE PERFECT) wird eher selten verwendet. Tipp: Werden Sie zuerst in allen anderen Zeiten sicher, bevor Sie sich diese Zeit ansehen.

> **!** Auch vom FUTURE PERFECT gibt es eine VERLAUFSFORM. Da diese aber noch seltener zur Anwendung kommt, sei hier nur darauf verwiesen, wie die Zeit gebildet wird:
>
> will + have + been + ing
>
> By the time you arrive, we will <u>have</u> been wai<u>ting</u> for ages!
>
> Wenn du ankommst, werden wir bereits eine Ewigkeit gewartet haben!

Going to Future

GEPLANT, ABSICHT – IRGENDWANN in der Zukunft
Das GOING TO FUTURE ist den meisten Lernenden bekannt, nicht immer aber die korrekte Anwendung. Manchmal wird vergessen, dass hinter dem going to *zwingend* ein INFINITIV stehen muss. Diese Zeit wird benutzt, um VORHABEN und PLÄNE in der Zukunft auszudrücken. Es kann sich dabei um konkrete Vorhaben oder unkonkrete Pläne handeln, meistens sind die Absichten ernst gemeint. Es drückt ebenso eine logische Schlussfolgerung hinsichtlich der Zukunft aus.
Beispiele:
What are you going to do after school?
I am probably going to study.
We are going to have a party this summer.
We are going to have a lot of fun.
Is she going to sell the house?
We are going to expand our sales activities this year.

Außerdem wird going to verwendet, wenn man etwas kommen sieht:
Vorsicht, Tom wirft gleich die Vase um.
Careful, Tom is going to break the vase!
Damn, we are going to miss the bus.
This is going to be really good.

Going to Future bilden

Aussage

Das going to ist eingebettet in die folgende Konstruktion:

is/are/am + going to + INFINITIV

Weil 1. ein -ing vorkommt, wird eine Form von to be benötigt, und weil 2. ein to vorkommt, muss ein INFINITIV folgen:

I	am	going to	<u>buy</u>	a new car soon.
You	are	going to	<u>get</u>	a great job, I know it.
He	is	going to	<u>go</u>	to America I fear.
She	is	going to	<u>find</u>	a boyfriend, don't worry.
It	is	going to	<u>get</u>	a new basket (the cat).
We	are	going to	<u>book</u>	this hotel again.
You	are	going to	<u>be</u>	bored by the film, I bet.
They	are	going to	<u>spend</u>	their next holiday in Holland.

Verneinung + not

I	am	not going to	<u>look</u>	for another job.
You	are	not going to	<u>give</u>	this up, are you?
She	is	not going to	<u>break</u>	up, never ever.
They	are	not going to	<u>find</u>	any compromise.

Frage – to be an Satzanfang

Am	I	going to	<u>get</u>	a second chance?
Are	you	going to	<u>give</u>	me another one?
Is	it	going to	<u>be</u>	difficult?
Are	we	going to	<u>like</u>	this?

Abkürzungen

I'm (not) going to
You're (not) going to
He's (not) going to
We're (not) going to
They're (not) going to

To go

Das Verb to go kann zweimal auftauchen, einmal im going to selbst und dann als VOLLVERB. Beispiel:

We are going to g<u>o</u> fishing, once dad has bought some new fishing rods.
You are not going to g<u>o</u> abroad, are you?

Going to Future in a nutshell

is/are/am/going to
+ INFINITIV

GEPLANT IRGENDWANN ABSICHT

Fragen, Unklarheiten, Notizen

Für die Sportfans –

GOING TO FUTURE in CRICKET-NEWS

"'We're going to need a bit of luck on a pitch like that,' said James Anderson, who claimed 3-47 in South Africa's second innings (Spielrunde)."

www.mirror.co.uk/sport/cricket

Beispielsätze Going to Future

We are not going to buy a new car this year.
Are you going to have a haircut this week?
Isn't he going to watch football tonight?
They are going to get a pet after the summer holidays.
I am definitely going to have a party when I pass the exam.

Present Continuous Future

ALLES ARRANGIERT – IN NAHER ZUKUNFT
Die Tatsache, dass PRESENT CONTINUOUS auch als Zukunftsform verwendet wird, ist den meisten Lernenden nicht bekannt. Im englischen Sprachgebrauch wird es jedoch häufig verwendet, und zwar immer, wenn etwas in naher Zukunft mit großer Sicherheit passiert. Das Kriterium ist, dass bereits Vorkehrungen und oft mit anderen Verabredungen getroffen wurden. Eben weil wir im Alltag häufig über Dinge sprechen, die in der nahen Zukunft passieren, kommt diese Form so oft vor. Die Verlaufsform wird gewählt, weil es Dinge sind, die zu einem Zeitpunkt in der Zukunft sehr sicher im Verlauf sein werden.
Beispiel:
Frage an die Freundin: Was hast du am Wochenende vor?
(Der Sprecher geht davon aus, dass die Freundin Vorkehrungen für das Wochenende getroffen hat.)
What are you doing at the weekend?
Antwort:
Tomorrow night I am meeting my sister at our parents' house.
On Saturday we are having lunch with the Cooks, who are in town.
But what about you? Are you seeing Paul tonight?
Die letzte Frage impliziert: Wenn sie Paul heute Abend trifft, dann haben die beiden sich sicher verabredet. Hätte man im Hinterkopf,

sie trifft sich spontan mit Paul, müsste die Frage stattdessen lauten:
Will you see Paul tonight?
Es bleibt immer auch eine Ermessens- und Empfindungssache, wie
wir fragen.

Present Continuous Future bilden

Aussage

Gebildet wird das PRESENT CONTINUOUS FUTURE genauso wie
das PRESENT CONTINUOUS (S. 44): mit einer Form von to be +
ing-Endung. Von der Form her lässt sich also nicht erkennen, ob es
sich um Gegenwart oder Zukunft handelt, das ergibt sich nur aus
dem Zusammenhang – wobei in Sätzen mit PRESENT CONTINUOUS
FUTURE häufig ein Zeitpunkt in der Zukunft genannt wird.

I	am	meeting	my parents tonight.	Zukunft
You	are	sitting	at the computer.	im Moment
He	is	collecting	her after school this afternoon.	Zukunft
She	is	cleaning	her teeth.	im Moment
It	is	coming	from England soon.	Zukunft
We	are	waiting	here.	im Moment
You	are	getting	a new car this summer.	Zukunft
They	are	behaving	well.	im Moment

Refresh:

VERNEINUNG + not hier: Zukunft

I	am not driving	down to Wales tonight.
You	are not watching	Superman again tonight!
He	is not leaving	the company next year.
They	are not seeing	each other for a long time then.

Frage am/is/are am **Satzanfang**

Am	I	meeting	you next week?
Is	she	buying	a house this month?
Are	we	having	a barbecue at the weekend?
Are	they	visiting	the United States this summer?

Abkürzungen

I'm (not) working this weekend.

You're (not) going out tonight.

He's (not) playing on Sunday.

We're (not) changing beds tonight.

They're (not) visiting Paul this week.

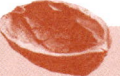

Present Continuous Future in a nutshell

is/am/are + ing

NAHE ZUKUNFT, FEST ABGEMACHT, SICHER,

VORKEHRUNGEN BEREITS GETROFFEN

Fragen, Unklarheiten, Notizen

Für die Sportfans –
PRESENT CONTINUOUS FUTURE in CYCLING-NEWS
"The UCI Track Cycling World Championships are coming to London's
Lee Valley VeloPark from Wednesday 2 to Sunday 6 March 2016."
www.britishcycling.org.uk/21January2016

Beispielsätze Present Continuous Future
We are meeting at Aurora's tonight at 8:30 pm.
Mother is coming from Brussels today.
Is Adam bringing his music?
They aren't going to the doctor during lunch because he feels better now.
I am seeing my friends at the weekend.
Susan is starting with piano lessons on Wednesday night.
As you are finishing could you please clear the table?
They are getting new furniture this week.
Her son is coming home for Easter.
He is going back on the 31st March.

Simple Present Future

FAHRPLÄNE, GENERELL GÜLTIG
SIMPLE PRESENT als Zukunftsform ist Fahrplänen und anderen exakten Zeitangaben vorbehalten. Zur Erinnerung: SIMPLE PRESENT steht für etwas Generelles, Regelmässiges – auch Fahrpläne gelten generell. Wenn jemand also sagen will, wann ein Flugzeug abfliegt, der Kinofilm am Abend anfängt, der Workshop beginnt und endet oder nach dem Bus fragt, verwendet er SIMPLE PRESENT:
Our plane leaves at 22 hours.
The film starts at 8 pm.
The workshop starts at 11 am and finishes at 19 hours.
When does the bus come?

Gebildet wird SIMPLE PRESENT FUTURE genauso wie das SIMPLE PRESENT (S. 30).

Refresh

Aussage

The bus/it	leav<u>es</u>	at 8 pm tonight.
The games/they	start	at 10 am tomorrow.

Verneinung + do/does + not + Infinitiv

It	does not/doesn't	start	until 11 pm.
They	do not/don't	arrive	before 9 pm at night.

Frage – do/does an Satzanfang + Infinitiv

Do<u>es</u>	it	start	at 8 pm?
Do	they	leave	on time?

Simple Present Future in a nutshell

INFINITIV, he/she/it + -s

FRAGE + VERNEINUNG mit do/does

FAHRPLÄNE, FESTE ZEITEN

Für die Sportfans –
SIMPLE PRESENT FUTURE in TENNIS-NEWS
"French Open 2016: Stan Wawrinka through as Richard Gasquet meets Andy Murray."
    www.bbc.com/sport/tennis

Beispielsätze Simple Present Future
The film starts at 20:30 tonight.
When does the party end?
What time does the train leave for Glasgow?
At which platform does it stop?
The plane is scheduled to take off with an hour delay.
School starts on 13th August.
We are back to school next Thursday.
The training begins on 20th September and goes on until the end of October.
The delivery is due to arrive by tonight.
The exam ends at 5 pm.

Um besser entscheiden zu können, wann nun genau WILL, GOING TO, PRESENT CONTINUOUS oder SIMPLE PRESENT FUTURE die richtige Wahl ist, um Zukunft bestmöglich auszudrücken, hier ein paar Beispiele hintereinander:

Das Telefon klingelt.
Peter, will you get it, please!   spontan

Wirst du morgen am Meeting teilnehmen?
Will you take part in the meeting tomorrow?   „wollen, vorhaben"

Ich werde auf dem Rückweg an der Apotheke anhalten.
I will drop in at the pharmacy on my way back.   Angebot

Nein, brauchst du nicht, Colin holt die Medizin heute Abend.
You don't have to. Colin is going to get the medicine tonight.   Plan

Vorsicht, du wirst die Flaschen mit deiner Tasche umwerfen.
Careful, you are going to knock over the bottles with your bag.

kommen sehen

Weiß er schon, was er nach der Schule machen will?
Does he know what he is going to do after school?   Plan, Absicht

Eins ist sicher: Er wird am Semesterende eine Party machen.
One thing is for sure: he is having his party at the end of the term.

Plan, arrangiert

Was machst du morgen Abend?
What are you doing tomorrow night?   fest geplant

Wann müssen wir da sein? Der Zug fährt um 8:15 ab.
When do we have to be there? The train leaves at 8:15.   Fahrplan

Tipp

Zusammenfassend kann man sagen: Es gibt oft mehrere Möglichkeiten, Zukunft auszudrücken. Wählt man eine Form, sollte man sie richtig anwenden. Zum Üben ist der beste Weg des Lernens das Ansehen und Hören von englischen Filmen sowie das Lesen von englischen Texten, wobei man dann genau hinhören bzw. hinschauen und sich fragen muss, warum hier genau diese Form gewählt wurde. Mit der Verbesserung des Sprachgefühls wächst mit der Zeit automatisch die Sicherheit zu entscheiden, welche FUTURE-Form am ehesten passt.

Praxis

It's your turn
Übung 22
SÄTZE mit FUTURE bilden

a. Wir fahren nächste Woche zu meiner Großtante nach Bayern.

---

b. Ich werde Sie anrufen, sobald ich die Unterlagen hier habe.

---

c. Wo werden Sie in zehn Jahren arbeiten?

---

d. Wann fängt das Kino an?

---

e. Will irgendjemand mitkommen zum Chinesen?

---

f. Morgen nach dem Frühstück fahren wir weiter nach Süden.

---

g. Was wirst du nach deiner Ausbildung machen?

---

h. Weißt du, was ich am Dienstag mache? Ich hole mein Auto ab.

Übung 23
PASSENDE FUTURE-FORM EINSETZEN

a. Perhaps he (to call) _____ me.

b. What time _____ he (to arrive) _____?

c. One of my colleagues (to retire) _____ next year.

d. It looks as if you (to need) _____ an umbrella
   later.

e. Careful – Tom (to throw) _____ the glass on
   the floor.

f. Next week this time I (to lie) _____ on the beach.

g. I (to send) _____ the manuscript at the end of
   the week.

h. Are you (to have) _____ a party this New Year's Eve?

Übung 24
RICHTIG EINSETZEN

a. Don't come after 6 pm – we (to have) _____
   dinner then. (WILL BE DOING FUTURE)

b. Sorry, I can't come, but I (to leave) _____
   tomorrow. (PRESENT CONTINUOUS FUTURE)

c. Where you (to buy) _____ new computer?

   I can recommend the shop on High Street. (GOING TO FUTURE)

d. I've just checked, the train (to leave) _____ from

   platform 4. (SIMPLE PRESENT FUTURE)

e. It's too hot. I (to call) _____ it a day.

   (WILL FUTURE)

f. (You, to see) _____ Alan tonight? (PRESENT

   CONTINUOUS FUTURE)

g. I (to work) _____ all summer to save some

   money. (WILL BE DOING FUTURE)

h. I have no idea what I (to do) _____ after school.

   (GOING TO FUTURE)

Konditionalsätze
Conditional I

IF-CLAUSE BEDINGUNG: FALLS A – DANN B

Die IF-SÄTZE sind nicht besonders beliebt, dabei sind sie einfach zu merken und anzuwenden. Das CONDITIONAL I beschreibt eine Bedingung mit einer Folge, das bedeutet, es ist unsicher, ob eine Sache eintrifft: *Falls* sie eintrifft, *dann* folgt daraus etwas!

If it rains tomorrow,   we will not/won't go to the zoo.
If it doesn't rain tomorrow, we will go to the zoo.

> **!** Einige nützliche Hilfestellungen zur Anwendung:
> A. Es gibt in der Regel ZWEI Satzteile.
> B. if darf NIE mit will in einem Satzteil stehen.
> C. Die Reihenfolge der Satzteile ist egal.
> D. if bedeutet „falls"
> E. if + SIMPLE PRESENT ⟷ will.

Conditional I bilden

AUSSAGE

Das CONDITIONAL I wird mit SIMPLE PRESENT gebildet und zwar in dem Teil des Satzes, in dem auch das if steht. Im anderen Satzteil steht will + INFINITIV. Die Bildung des SIMPLE PRESENT folgt der Regel: bei he, she, it mit -s, bei Verneinung mit do/does (S. 30).

if + SIMPLE PRESENT	will
If I find a good job this week	I will give a party at the weekend.
If you don't take an umbrella	you will get wet.
If he doesn't get a pay-rise	will I?
If she doesn't stop bossing him	she will make him leave her.
If it snows	we will go skiing spontaneously.
If we find a house	we will be so happy.
If I promise no homework	will you be quiet?
If they carry on like this	they will never succeed.

Can, Must, Shall, Befehl

Statt will kann auch ein MODALVERB can, must, shall stehen oder ein IMPERATIV = BEFEHL:

If I am not back soon	you can follow me.	Modalverb
If he doesn't sign the contract	you must talk to him.	Modalverb
If they don`t shut up	we shall not finish early.	Modalverb
If I don't call within an hour	shut the door.	Befehl

When

Manchmal wird if mit when verwechselt, allerdings ändert sich in dem Fall die Bedeutung, denn when heißt „sobald" und nicht „falls".

When I arrive in London	I will call you.	sobald
When he arrives	please collect him, will you?	sobald
If he arrives	please offer him accommodation.	falls

Conditional I in a nutshell

if + SIMPLE PRESENT SATZTEIL I

will oder HILFSVERB + INFINITIV SATZTEIL II

Wenn A, dann folgt daraus B

NIE if + will in EINEM SATZTEIL

Fragen, Unklarheiten, Notizen

Für die Sportfans –
CONDITIONAL I in FOOTBALL-NEWS
(Mesud Özil's transfer contract Real Madrid to Arsenal): "The clause reads: 'If at any time whilst the Player is employed by Buyer ... Buyer intends to transfer the registration of the Player ... to another professional football club ..., Buyer shall promptly notify Seller in writing ..."

www.dailymail.co.uk/sport/football/article-3415596

Beispielsätze Conditional I
If you are not home by 9 pm, we won't have your party.
If I don't find a job soon, I'll be broke.
They will find a nice house, if they try hard enough.
If we all work together, the project will become a great success.
If you don't accept my proposal, you can just go.

Conditional II

IF-CLAUSE ... STELL DIR VOR, ICH WÄRE ... HYPOTHESE
Hypothesen sind unbewiesene Annahmen. Anders als beim CONDITIONAL I geht es beim CONDITIONAL II nicht einfach nur um Bedingung und Folge, sondern um eine hypothetische Bedingung und deren mögliche Folge: *Wenn ... wäre, dann würde ... Oder: Stell dir vor, ich wäre ... (bin ich aber nicht).*
Beispiel:
Wenn ich Millionär wäre, würde ich meinen Job kündigen.
If I was a millionaire, I would quit my job.
Wenn er einen Unfall hätte, würden wir uns um seine Familie kümmern.
If he had an accident, we would care for his family.

> ❗ Wie man diese Sätze konstruiert, lernt man am besten einfach auswendig und hält sich dabei ganz stur an folgende Vorgaben. Andernfalls kommt man nicht weiter, denn hier lässt sich kaum etwas wörtlich übersetzen!
> A. Es gibt in der Regel wieder ZWEI Satzteile.
> B. if darf NIE mit would in einem Satzteil stehen.
> C. Die Reihenfolge der Satzteile ist egal.
> D. if + SIMPLE PAST ←——→ would.

Conditional II bilden

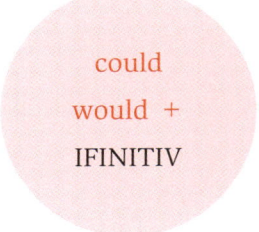

could

would +

IFINITIV

Aussage

CONDITIONAL II wird mit SIMPLE PAST gebildet, und zwar in dem Teil des Satzes, in dem auch das if steht. Im anderen Satzsteil steht would + INFINITIV. Die Bildung von SIMPLE PAST (S. 71):

if + SIMPLE PAST	would
If I didn't have a job	I would find myself one.
If you found 100 Euros in the street	would you keep them?
If he got up ten minutes earlier	he would not/wouldn't be late.
If she had a brother	she would teach him chess.
If it didn't snow	we wouldn't come here.

If we had more money	we <u>could</u> stop behaving so jealously.
If you sent me the letter	I <u>could</u> have a look at it.
If they won the lottery	they <u>would</u> stay normal people.

Mit could funktioniert es genauso. Es heißt dann „könnte" anstatt „würde".

Conditional II in a nutshell

if + 2. FORM   SATZTEIL I

would/could + INFINITIV   SATZTEIL II

HYPOTHESE Was wäre, wenn …

NIE if + would in EINEM SATZTEIL!

Fragen, Unklarheiten, Notizen

Für die Sportfans –
CONDITIONAL II in ROWING-NEWS

"If ever an international rowing event belonged to any nation, the women's quadruple sculls (Doppelvierer) would belong to Germany."
    www.worldrowing.com/news/united-states-disruption-germany

Beispielsätze Conditional II
We would join you if we had the time, which we haven't.
If you were a little younger, I would take you out tonight.
He wouldn't feel so sad for himself if he looked at it realistically.
We would get a nice little flat in Paris if we won the lottery.
They wouldn't mind if he sold the house next door.
If I found gold I could live a rich man's life.

Conditional III

IF-CLAUSE – WAS HÄTTE SEIN KÖNNEN (PAST)
Das CONDITIONAL III brauchen wir, wenn wir sagen wollen, was zu einem bestimmten Zeitpunkt in der Vergangenheit alles hätte sein können. Auch hier wird also eine Hypothese formuliert: Wir stellen uns etwas vor, das aber nicht eingetroffen ist.

Beispiel:
Wenn ich in der Schule nicht so faul gewesen wäre, was hätte nicht aus mir werden können!
If I hadn't been so lazy at school, imagine what I could have achieved!
Stell dir vor, was hätte passieren können, wenn der Falschfahrer auf ihrer Autobahn gewesen wäre!
Imagine what could have happened if the wrong-way driver had been on their motorway!

! Es sind solche Sätze, vor denen viele kapitulieren. Es ist in der Tat nicht ganz einfach und im Sprachalltag wird diese Zeit nicht allzu häufig benutzt, trotzdem: Wenn man das kann, hat man einen großen Schritt zu gutem Englisch geschafft – und wird so manchen damit beeindrucken.

Conditional III bilden

Diese Sätze funktionieren so:

IN EINEM SATZTEIL	IM ANDEREN SATZTEIL
If + PAST PERFECT	would/could + PRESENT PERFECT
If + had been	would/could + have become

Die Reihenfolge der Satzteile ist wie bei allen CONDITIONAL-SÄTZEN beliebig:

If + PAST PERFECT (S. 89)	would + PRESENT PERFECT (S. 53)
If she had arrived earlier	we would have had more time.
If they hadn't lost their car	they would/could have stayed.

would + PRESENT PERFECT	if + PAST PERFECT
Would I have been named Alex	if I had been a boy?
He could have come	if they had known you had a party.

Conditional III in a nutshell

if + had + 3. FORM   SATZTEIL I

would + have + 3. FORM   SATZTEIL II

HYPOTHESE Was wäre gewesen, wenn …

NIE if + would in EINEM SATZTEIL!

Praxis

It's your Turn
Übung 25
CONDITIONAL I, II oder III?

a. You will smell if you (not to change) _____ your clothes.

b. What (you, to do) _____ if you heard the alarm?

c. We'll have to walk if we (to run out) _____ of petrol here.

d. There (not to be) _____ so many accidents if the people drove more carefully.

e. If you shake that bottle, it (not to be) _____ easy to drink.

f. If you (to wear) _____ this hat, nobody would have recognized you.

g. If you get the driving license today, we (to celebrate) _____.

h. I wouldn't have brought the children if I (to know) _____ that your children weren't in.

Übung 26
SÄTZE BILDEN mit CONDITIONAL

a. Ich werde richtig sauer, wenn du nicht sofort herkommst.

_____

b. Hätte ich damals mal auf euch gehört, dann wäre es mir besser ergangen.

_____

c. Stell dir mal vor, wir hätten so viel Geld, was würden wir dann machen?

_____

d. Wir gehen zur Party, wenn es dort Essen gibt.

_____

e. Wenn er nicht so jähzornig wäre, wäre es nett, mit ihm zu arbeiten.

_____

f. Die Firma hätte nicht überlebt, wenn sie nicht an die Börse gegangen wäre.

_____

g. Wenn du dreimal klingelst, weiß ich, dass du es bist.

_____

h. Wäre der Garten größer, hätten wir viel mehr zu tun.

_____

Übung 27
SÄTZE im CONDITIONAL BILDEN

a. CONDITIONAL I

If the new secretary (to be) _____ good, we (to

offer) _____ her a long-term contract.

b. CONDITIONAL II

If they (to be) _____ younger, they surely (not to

complain) _____ so much about the noise.

c. CONDITIONAL III

If I (to know) _____ it earlier, I (to send)

_____ an email to everyone.

d. CONDITIONAL I

We (to go) _____ to the theatre, if they (to get)

_____ tickets.

e. CONDITIONAL II

It (to be) _____ crazy if we (to win)

_____ the lottery.

Zeiten wiederholen – Sätze deklinieren

Diese Übung eignet sich hervorragend dazu, sich die Zeitformen besser einzuprägen. Alle Sätze werden im Folgenden stur durchdekliniert, also in jede Zeitform gebracht. Das ist mechanisch, hat aber bleibenden Effekt. Dabei geht es *nicht* um den Sinn – denn es entstehen zwangsläufig sinnfreie Sätze. Es kommt allein auf das Üben an. Insgesamt müssen pro deutschem Satz 15 englische Sätze gebildet werden, wobei PRESENT CONTINUOUS und SIMPLE PRESENT je zweimal vorkommen (GEGENWART + ZUKUNFT).

BEISPIEL: Das Ei sieht gut aus.

SIMPLE PRESENT		The egg	looks	good.
PRESENT CONTINUOUS		The egg	is looking	good.
PRESENT PERFECT		The egg	has looked	good.
PRESENT PERFECT CONTINUOUS		The egg	has been looking	good.
SIMPLE PAST		The egg	looked	good.
PAST PERFECT		The egg	had looked	good.
PAST PERFECT CONTINUOUS		The egg	had been looking	good.
PAST CONTINUOUS		The egg	was looking	good.
FUTURE WILL		The egg	will look	good.
FUTURE GOING TO		The egg	is going to look	good.
FUTURE CONTINUOUS		The egg	is looking	good.
FUTURE SIMPLE PRESENT		The egg	looks	good.
COND. I	If you find an egg	it will look	good.
COND. II	If you found an egg	it would look	good.
COND. III	If you had found an egg	it would have looked	good.

BEISPIEL: Das Leben ist großartig.

SIMPLE PRESENT	Life	is	great.
PRESENT CONTINUOUS	Life	is being	great.
PRESENT PERFECT	Life	has been	great.
PRESENT PERFECT CONTINUOUS	Life	has been being	great.
SIMPLE PAST	Life	was	great.
PAST PERFECT	Life	had been	great.
PAST PERFECT CONTINUOUS	Life	had been being	great.
PAST CONTINUOUS	Life	was being	great.
FUTURE WILL	Life	will be	great.
FUTURE GOING TO	Life	is going to be	great.
FUTURE CONTINUOUS	Life	is being	great.
FUTURE SIMPLE PRESENT	Life	is	great.
COND. I	If you look at it	life will be	great.
COND. II	If you looked at it	life would be	great.
COND. III	If you had looked at it	life would have been	great.

Praxis

It's your turn
Übung 28
DEKLINIEREN: Wir wohnen in Hamburg.

SIMPLE PRESENT _____

PRESENT CONTINUOUS _____

PRESENT PERFECT _____

PRESENT PERFECT CONTINUOUS _____

SIMPLE PAST _____

PAST PERFECT _____

PAST PERFECT CONTINUOUS _____

PAST CONTINUOUS _____

FUTURE WILL _____

FUTURE GOING TO _____

FUTURE CONTINUOUS _____

FUTURE SIMPLE PRESENT _____

CONDITIONAL I   If we want to … _____

CONDITIONAL II _____

CONDITIONAL III _____

Übung 29
DEKLINIEREN: Er mag Tiere.

SIMPLE PRESENT _____

PRESENT CONTINUOUS _____

PRESENT PERFECT _____

PRESENT PERFECT CONTINUOUS _____

SIMPLE PAST _____

PAST PERFECT _____

PAST PERFECT CONTINUOUS _____

PAST CONTINUOUS _____

FUTURE WILL _____

FUTURE GOING TO _____

FUTURE CONTINUOUS _____

FUTURE SIMPLE PRESENT _____

CONDITIONAL I   If he can _____

CONDITIONAL II _____

CONDITIONAL III _____

Übung 30
DEKLINIEREN: Das ist einfach.

SIMPLE PRESENT _____

PRESENT CONTINUOUS _____

PRESENT PERFECT _____

PRESENT PERFECT CONTINUOUS _____

SIMPLE PAST _____

PAST PERFECT _____

PAST PERFECT CONTINUOUS _____

PAST CONTINUOUS _____

FUTURE WILL _____

FUTURE GOING TO _____

FUTURE CONTINUOUS _____

FUTURE SIMPLE PRESENT _____

CONDITIONAL I   If you look at it _____

CONDITIONAL II _____

CONDITIONAL III _____

TEIL DREI
Damit wird es komplett

There is + there are = es gibt

| there is | = | es gibt (eine/einen) | Singular/Einzahl |
| there are | = | es gibt (mehrere) | Plural/Mehrzahl |

There is a cafe over there.
There is a lot to do before the visitors arrive.
There is nothing left to say.
There are three free tables in the café.
There are more boys than girls in the class.
There are several hundred countries in the world.

Verneinung + Frage

There is not/isn't a single chair left.	Verneinung
Is there a seat left for grandma?	Frage
There isn't much poppy seed in the muffin.	Verneinung
Is there anything left from lunch?	Frage

There are not/aren't many people in the club tonight.	Verneinung
Are there toilets in this shop at all?	Frage
There aren't any sharks in the aquarium.	Verneinung
Are there any doctors aboard this aircraft?	Frage

Pronomen ich, du, er, sie, es

Pronomen sind Fürwörter, sie stehen stellvertretend für ein oder mehrere vorerwähnte Personen oder Dinge. Es gibt mehrere Untergruppen. Die Grundformen des sogenannten Personalpronomens sind die Folgenden:

EINZAHL		MEHRZAHL	
I	ich	we	wir
you	du	you	ihr
he/she/it	er	they	sie

Die Grundform wird verwendet, wenn das Fürwort an der SUBJEKTSTELLE eines Satzes steht:

Mr. Jones	buys	a book.
He	buys	a book.

Wenn wir dagegen a book durch ein Fürwort ersetzen wollen, steht das Pronomen an der OBJEKTSTELLE des Satzes: Mr. Jones buys it. Dann müssen diese Formen verwendet werden:

me	mir, mich
you	dir, dich
him/her/it	ihm/ihn, ihr/sie, ihm/es
us	uns
you	euch
them	ihnen, sie

Zwei weitere Untergruppen brauchen wir, wenn es um Besitz geht. In der ersten Gruppe steht das Fürwort wie ein Adjektiv vor dem Hauptwort:

Das sind *schöne* Schuhe.	These are beautiful shoes.	Adjektiv
Das sind *unsere* Schuhe.	These are our shoes.	Fürwort

Die Formen sind in diesem Fall:

my	mein(e)
your	dein(e)

his/her/its	sein(e)/ihr(e)/sein(e)
our	unser(e)
your	euer (eure)
their	ihre

In der zweiten Gruppe steht das Fürwort selbst für = ersetzt das Hauptwort (in der Fachsprache sagt man: Es wird pronominal benutzt, nicht adjektivisch wie in der ersten Gruppe):

These are my shoes.   These (shoes) are mine.

This is our room.   This (room) is ours.

Die Formen sind in diesem Fall – unabhängig ob Einzahl oder Mehrzahl verwendet wird:

Mine	meins, meine	This bag is mine.	These socks are mine.
yours	deins, deine	This chair is yours.	The tablets over there are yours.
his	seins, seine	This book is his.	The trees are his, he cuts them.
hers	ihrs, ihre	The ring is hers.	The ear-rings are hers, too.
its	seins, seine	The basket is its.	The toys are its.
ours	unsere(s)	This trolly is ours.	These suitcases are ours.
yours	euers, eure	Is this garden yours?	Are the trees yours?
theirs	ihr, ihre	The shed is theirs.	The clothes are theirs, too.

Apostroph 's

Das s mit APOSTROPH ('s) für eine Besitzanzeige kommt im Englischen sehr häufig vor (es wird auch im Deutschen benutzt, z.B. in „Gabi's Hundesalon" oder „Uli's Kiosk", ist aber ein Anglizismus und eigentlich falsch). Der Apostroph ersetzt in diesem Fall keinen Buchstaben und das s kein Wort, es hat nur eine FUNKTION. Will man auf 's verzichten, muss man im Englischen den Satz anders bilden:

a.   This is Henry's dog.   This is the dog of Henry.
b.   Sheela is the Smiths' cat.   Sheela is the cat of the Smiths.

BEACHTE: Bei a. gehört der Hund nur einer Person (Henry), bei b. gehört die Katze mehreren Personen (der gesamten Familie Smith). In diesem Fall steht das Wort the Smiths schon im Plural. Hier noch ein 's anzuhängen, könnte niemand aussprechen, daher reicht der Apostroph. Im Deutschen würden wir sagen: Das sind die Kinder von den Müllers. Im Englischen heißt es:

These are the Müllers' children.

Außerdem kann das 's Wörter abkürzen (Erläuterungen nachfolgend):

c.   Henry's a nice boy.
d.   Henry's looking very interested.
e.   He's got a nice mountain bike.
f.   Henry's had a bad dream tonight.
g.   Let's have a coffee.

Zu c. Der zweithäufigste Fall: 's ersetzt das is in der Form von to be:

Henry's (is) a nice boy.   Henry ist ein netter Junge.
The cat's (is) really cute.   Die Katze ist wirklich süß.

Zu d. Hier steht das 's für is im PRESENT CONTINUOUS:

Henry's (is) looking very interested.   Henry schaut interessiert.
It's (is) raining cats and dogs.   Es regnet wie aus Kübeln.

Zu e. 's ersetzt hier has im SIMPLE PRESENT und kommt daher nur in Verbindung mit der 3. Person Singular he, she, it vor.

Henry's (has) got a nice bike.   Henry hat ein schönes Rad.
Lisa's (has) got many friends.   Lisa hat viele Freundinnen.
It's (has) got a broken leg.   (Die Katze) hat ein
                                    gebrochenes Bein.

Zu f. Auch hier ersetzt 's das has, aber im PRESENT PERFECT, auch hier nur in Verbindung mit der 3. Person Singular he, she oder it:

Henry's (has) had a bad dream.   Henry hat heute Nacht
                                    schlecht geträumt.
Mother's (has) fetched the milk.   Mutter hat die Milch abgeholt.

Zu g. Hier steht 's für us (uns). Dabei ist ohne den Kontext nicht zu entscheiden, ob die Aussage an zwei oder mehr Personen gerichtet ist.

Let's (let us) have a coffee.   Lass (oder: Lasst) uns
                                    einen Kaffee trinken.
Let's (let us) cook together.   Lass (oder: Lasst) uns
                                    gemeinsam kochen.

Apostroph 'd 'll 'm 're 't 've

Neben dem Apostroph s gibt es noch andere Abkürzungen mit Apostroph im Englischen – hier eine Übersicht:

'D =   HAD + WOULD

Zur Unterscheidung: Auf had folgt die 3. FORM = PARTIZIP PERFEKT, hinter would steht immer ein INFINITIV.

We'd (had) seen the film earlier.
We'd (had) been there three years before.
You'd (would) enjoy it, too.
They'd (would) go with us eventually.

'll = will

He'll tell me later, I know.
You'll get a pay rise next autumn.
We'll stay here then?

'm = am

I'm sixteen years old and I'm from London.

're = are

You're not from here, are you?
Careful, they're hot.
You're my best friend.

't = not

Auch bei Verneinungen kann abgekürzt werden. Hier wird allerdings auch zusammengezogen, das n aus not kommt an das vorausgegangene Hilfsverb und das Apostroph steht lediglich für das o, so wird aus do not – don't, aus cannot – can't, aus have not – haven't und aus has not – hasn't:
We don't think this is a good idea.
He can't come to the party.
We haven't got a clue.
She hasn't brushed her teeth.
Im Fall von will not wird eine Änderung vorgenommen. Hieraus wird won't:
They won't come to the church.
Won't you try at least?

've = have

They've got a house on the beach.
I've had a good party.
You've done me a lot of good.
We've had enough of this.

Beispielsätze für Apostroph

I've had enough of this, let's put it aside.
The Robinsons' house is being sold.
Henry's mother and sister are really miserable people.
You're far too young to be let in here.
We're such fools.
I'm back in a second.
If he doesn't watch it, he'll get beaten up.
He'd been married before but I don't know how long or to whom.

Artikel a + an + the

Im Englischen gibt es
a) den unbestimmten Artikel   a + an   ein/eine/ein
b) den bestimmten Artikel   the   der/die/das

Unbestimmter Artikel a, an

Wann a oder an? Aus Gründen der Aussprache wird an verwendet, wenn ein VOKAL = a, e, i, o oder u folgt, also:
My father has (got) a wife and a house and a car.
BUT: This boy has (got) an apple and an umbrella.
An wird auch verwendet, wenn ein stummer KONSONANT + VOKAL folgt, z.B. bei hour – hier bleit das h stumm, also:
We meet in an hour.

Vor Zeitangaben

Vor Zeit- und Maßangaben bedeuten a/an = per, pro oder je.
I do exercises four times a week.
We cannot go on holiday three times a year.
The tomatoes are 3.45 Euros a kilo.
He has to measure the water level three times an hour.

A/an steht immer vor Berufsbezeichnungen und Nationalitäten (anders als im Deutschen):

He's a journalist.	Er ist Journalist.
She is a cook.	Sie ist Köchin.
He is an American.	Er ist Amerikaner.
Aber: He is American.	Er ist amerikanisch.
She is a Greek.	Griechin
She is Greek.	griechisch

Bestimmter Artikel the

Das Besondere am unbestimmten englischen Artikel ist, dass es keine Unterscheidung zwischen der, die, das gibt, was es für den Lernenden einfach macht:

„der/die"	„die"	„das/die"	
the man	the woman	the house	Singular
the men	the women	the houses	Plural

Auch bei the verändert sich etwas, wenn das folgende Wort mit VOKAL beginnt, zwar nicht in der Schreib-, wohl aber in der Sprechweise. Aus einem kurzen e wird ein langes ie:

The tree stands in the garden.	kurzes e
The umbrella is not open.	langes ie

Verwendet wird der bestimmte Artikel immer dann, wenn der Sprecher an eine bestimmte Situation oder Sache denkt. Ohne den Artikel geht es dagegen, wenn etwas Allgemeines ausgedrückt wird. Ob etwas bestimmt oder unbestimmt ist, hängt davon ab, was der Sprecher sagen will.

School is boring.	unbestimmt	Schule „an sich" ist langweilig.
The school is boring.	bestimmt	Der Sprecher denkt an seine Schule.

Reading is fun.	unbestimmt	Lesen „an sich" macht Spaß.
The reading went very slowly.	bestimmt	Der Sprecher denkt an eine konkrete Situation.
People go to church.	unbestimmt	„Generell" gehen Menschen in die Kirche.
People go to the church.	bestimmt	Sie gehen in eine bestimmte Kirche.
Skiing is difficult.	unbestimmt	Schifahren ist „generell" schwer.
The skiing was great.	bestimmt	Der Sprecher denkt an einen bestimmten Schiurlaub.

Generell

Der bestimmte Artikel the steht generell vor:

Familiennamen und Ländernamen im Plural.
The Smiths are going on holiday tomorrow.
The Meyers are having a party tonight.
We are going to the USA (United States of America).
We spent our last holiday in the Netherlands.

Gebirgen, Regionen und Inselgruppen.
Did you visit the Rocky Mountains when you were in the USA?
Pakistan lies in the Middle East.
The Bahamas were very nice.
We like to spend winter in the Canaries.

Namen mit of, Ozeanen und Flüssen.
In New York we visited the Statue of Liberty.
My aunt lives on the Isle of Wight.
Düsseldorf is located on the Rhine.

Aber: Aufgepasst bei der Nennung von Straßen, Seen, Parks mit Eigennamen – da es den Central Park u. ä. nur einmal gibt, kommt er ohne the aus.

We crossed Central Park on our way to the hotel.
She lives near Lake Michigan.
We live in Oxford Street.

Bei den Jahreszeiten ist beides möglich, mit oder ohne the.
We often have a barbecue in (the) summer.
In (the) spring I am going to paint the windows.
Ausnahme USA: the fall

Praxis

It's your turn
Übung 31
MIT THE oder OHNE?

a. I like _____ pop music.

b. We all are afraid of _____ death of the ones we love.

c. The book vividly describes _____ life of _____ poor people

in _____ medieval England.

d. If you wish to succeed in _____ life, you must learn how to

act well.

e. With _____ exception of _____ dinner we spent all meals

together.

f. _____ family is very important to me.

g. When _____ going gets tough, _____ tough get going.

h. _____ feeling was very strange.

Übung 32

MIT THE oder A/AN oder OHNE?

a. Wir waren letztes Jahr im Winter auf den Malediven.

_____

b. Die Schule, die Karl besucht, macht im Sommer drei Wochen zu.

_____

c. Müllers wohnen in der High Street Nummer 12.

_____

d. Deutschland hat nur einen hohen Berg – die Zugspitze.

_____

e. Er ist Automechaniker.

_____

f. Sie ist Portugiesin.

_____

g. Korfu ist eine Insel im Ionischen Meer.

_____

h. Erinnerst du dich an den Montag, als du gefeuert wurdest?

_____

Plural = Mehrzahl

Bei der Bildung von Mehrzahl = Plural wird ein -s an das Hauptwort = Nomen = noun angehängt.

book	books
shoe	shoes

Wörter, die auf sogenannte Zischlaute wie -ss, -ch, -s, -sh, -x enden, bekommen ein -es angehängt.

glass	glasses
watch	watches
gas	gases
dish	dishes
box	boxes

Wörter, die auf -y enden, bei denen vor dem -y aber ein Konsonant steht, enden auf -ies.

fly	flies
ly	lies

Steht vor dem -y aber ein Vokal a, e, i, o, u, dann wird einfach ein -s angehängt

play	plays
boy	boys

Daneben gibt es Wörter mit unregelmässigem Plural, die man lernen muss, z. B.:

foot	feet
man	men
mouse	mice
woman	women
sheep	sheep
tooth	teeth

Außerdem existieren Wörter ohne Plural, die *immer* im Singular verwendet werden oder trotz einer Pluralform (Beispiel: news) als Singular behandelt werden:

They didn't get any aid.	keine Hilfe/Unterstützung
There was no evidence.	es gab keine Beweise
They had a lot of homework.	viele Hausaufgaben
Let the music play.	Musik
No news is good news.	keine Nachricht = gute Nachricht

Dinge, die aus zwei gleichen Teilen bestehen, sind sogenannte PAIR NOUNS und stehen *immer* im Plural, es sei denn man setzt a pair of davor, z. B.:

glasses	die Brille = zwei Gläser
a pair of glasses	
trousers	die Hose = zwei Hosenbeine
a pair of trousers	

Beispiel:
Where are my jeans?
I am sure I put a fresh pair of jeans on your chair. Is it not there?

Sammelbegriffe wie government, staff, family können als Singualr ODER Plural verwendet werden, je nachdem was man betonen will: einzelne Mitglieder oder die gesamte Gruppe.
The government want to increase taxes.
                    Betonung auf den Mitgliedern der Regierung
The government wants to increase taxes.
                    Betonung auf der „Gesamtregierung"
The staff don't agree with the new working hours.   jedes Mitglied
The staff doesn't agree with the working hours.
                    die Belegschaft „als solche"
My family, which are down in California, is very big.
My family, which is in Calais, is rather small.

Achtung: police benötigt *immer* ein Verb im Plural:
The police have arrested the thief.
The police are increasingly getting under pressure.

Ordinalzahlen

Unter Ordinalzahlen versteht man die Ordnungszahlen erstens, zweitens, drittens etc. Für die Zahlen 1–3 (auch 21–23, 31–33 etc.) gibt es eigene Endungen:

1	-st	= first	1st of October, 21st December
2	-nd	= second	32nd chapter, 52nd row
3	-rd	= third	3rd of April, 53rd round

An alle anderen Zahlen wird -th angehängt:
fourth, fifth (Schreibweise beachten, das e entfällt), sixth, seventh, eighth, ninth (Schreibweise beachten, das e entfällt), tenth, fourteenth etc.
Achtung: 11, 12 und 13 fallen unter -th:
eleventh, twelfth, thirteenth

Da das -th für uns nicht so einfach auszusprechen ist, kommen die Ordinalzahlen oft als Zungenbrecher (tongue twister) daher:
The twenty-fifth meeting of the thirty-third regiment ended in a disaster for the fourteenth time!

> **!** SEHENSWERT: So schwierig auszusprechende Sätze hat schon Loriot zum Anlass für seinen Sketch „Die Inhaltsangabe" genommen (mit Evelyn Hamann):
> https://www.youtube.com/watch?v = ZygK3yvUee4
> (2:45 Minuten)

Im Zusammenhang mit den Ordinalzahlen weise ich Schüler in der Regel auf das Folgende hin, und zwar wie im Englischen *einmal, zweimal, dreimal* usw. ausgedrückt wird:

once	einmal
twice	zweimal
three times	dreimal – und von hier an immer so weiter
four times	viermal etc.
twenty times	zwanzigmal
a hundred times	hundertmal

Teacher: I will say it once or twice, but I will not repeat it a hundred times!

Hauptwörter / Nomen / nouns

Anders als im Deutschen werden Hauptwörter im Englischen generell klein geschrieben (small letters). Groß geschrieben (capital letters) werden lediglich Namen, also Eigennamen, Wochentage, Nationalitäten, aber auch Titel. Die Regel ist einfach, trotzdem ergeben sich in der Praxis viele Fehler:

CAPITAL LETTERS: Monday, Tuesday, Wednesday, Thursday, Friday, Saturday, Sunday, Christmas Day (25.12.), Boxing Day (26.12.), New Year's Eve (31.12.), New Year's Day (1.1.), March, April, etc., Germany, German, Italy, Italian, America, American, the Queen, King George.

Some + any

Bei der Verwendung von some = etwas/einige und any = irgendetwas/irgendwelche kommen Verwechslungen vor. Dabei gibt es zwei klare und EINFACHE REGELN:

1. some bei AUSSAGEN, BITTEN und ANGEBOTEN!

There are some apples in the bowl.	Aussage
Could you please lend me some money?	Bitte
Can I have some of these apples please?	Bitte
Would you like some tea?	Angebot

2. any bei FRAGEN und VERNEINUNG!

Are there any apples left?	Frage
Have you any fruit at all?	Frage
Unfortunately we haven't (got) any tea!	Verneinung
There aren`t any children here.	Verneinung

Dasselbe gilt für zusammengesetzte Worte:

something	–	anything
somebody	–	anybody
someone	–	anyone
somewhere	–	anywhere

We will find something nice for her.	Aussage
Have you anything to declare?	Frage
We haven't anything to eat.	Verneinung
I hope you will find someone special.	Aussage
Have you met anyone you know?	Frage
He doesn't know anyone at all.	Verneinung

Some + any können für ein Hauptwort stehen, wenn es nicht wiederholt werden soll:

Have they got the sneakers we have been looking for?
Yes, they have some (sneakers) size 7.
No they haven't got any (sneakers) at all.

Much + many

Much + many haben die gleiche Bedeutung: viel/e. Der Unterschied: Much wird verwendet für alles, was *nicht zählbar* ist, many dagegen für alles, was *zählbar* ist. Als zählbar gelten dabei wirklich nur einzelne Stücke oder Einheiten. Geld (als Oberbegriff) beispielsweise lässt sich nicht zählen. Zählen kann man nur die Einheiten (Euros, Dollar) und die Münzen. Much kann man auch durch a lot ersetzen, wenn es für ein Hauptwort steht:

How much money have you got?	I haven't got much/a lot.
How many dollars have you got?	I have twenty dollars.
How many coins are there?	Four coins.

Beispiele:
Much bei: milk, marmalade, time, patience, energy
There isn't much more marmalade in the jar.
How much time have you got today?
She has much patience with the children.
He hasn't got much energy left.

Many bei: bottles of milk, jars of marmalade, Euros, minutes, apples, pears
How many bottles of milk are there left?
How many jars of marmalade shall I buy?
How many Euros does it cost?
How many minutes will it take?

(a) little + (a) few

Entsprechendes gilt für (a) little + (a) few (wenig/e). Für *nicht Zählbares* werden a little = ein wenig oder little = wenig verwendet, für *Zählbares* nehmen wir a few = wenige/ein paar.

I have only a little money in the bank.
She gets little support from her husband.
The children have little understanding for her situation.
There is a little food left from last night's supper.

I have only a few dollars left.
Could you listen to me for a few minutes please?
When we tidied our room we found a few pieces we had forgotten about.
They have few problems.

QUITE A FEW = etliche, mehrere
Achtung Falle: In Zusammensetzung mit a few hat das Wörtchen quite eine verstärkende Bedeutung und aus *wenigen* werden *etliche/mehrere*!
There were quite a few people at the party.
It took us quite a few minutes to get in.
The company was having quite a few problems.
Quite a few of us were not happy with the situation.

Praxis

It's your turn
Übung 33
RICHTIG EINSETZEN
any/some, any-/something, any-/someone, any-/somewhere

a. I am not going _____ with you!

b. Let's get _____ stamps to put on the cards.

c. Do you know _____ songs by Michael Jackson?

d. There is _____ I must tell you!

e. Can _____ please bring me the plates?

f. I have heard they haven't found _____ in the house.

g. _____ over the rainbow.

h. Does _____ know the family across the street?

Übung 34
SÄTZE BILDEN mit MUCH, MANY, LITTLE, (A) FEW

a. Ich kenne noch viele Freunde von früher aus meiner Schulzeit.

_____

b. Wie viel Mut es braucht, um Bungee Jumping zu machen!

_____

c. Jakob hat heute so wenig gegessen!

_____

d. Wir sind nur ganz wenige Male nicht zum Sport gegangen.

_____

e. Da waren schon eine ganze Menge Leute.

_____

f. Es war wenig Verkehr auf den Straßen heute.

_____

g. Wir waren oft bei ihnen zu Hause zum Essen.

_____

h. Viel Lärm um Nichts.

_____

Imperativ, Aufforderung, Befehl

Die Befehlsform oder Aufforderung im Englischen = IMPERATIV ist
sehr einfach: Es ist der INFINITIV = GRUNDFORM des Verbs. Da-
runter fallen auch Anweisungen, beispielsweise in Formularen, Prü-
fungsaufgaben:
Sign at the bottom.
Leave me alone!
Get us some milk please.
Be here at 7 p.m.
Go and help your father!
Let's see what we can do.
Let us have another coffee.
Come on, get going!
Shut up!

Häufig wird in der Werbung so formuliert oder man liest Aufforde-
rungen in öffentlichen Räumen:

Have **a break, have a KitKat!**

Come **in and find out!**

Mind **the gap!**

Hop **on, hop off**

Verneinungen werden wie im SIMPLE PRESENT mit don't = do not
gebildet. Im Imperativ gibt es kein doesn't (für die 3. Person), denn
es werden immer nur Personen direkt angesprochen, also immer you
(du/ihr).
Do not/don't throw the things there!
Do not/don't get wet!
Do not/don't stop having fun.

Used to

To use beutet „benutzen, verwenden", aber **used to** hat eine andere, eigene Bedeutung, nämlich: Früher habe ich etwas regelmäßig oder dauerhaft getan (aber heute tue ich das nicht mehr).
I used to live in Hamburg, but now I live in Berlin.
We used to meet the Scotts regularly, but we don't any more.
The gym used to open on Sundays, but it doesn't any longer.
Der zweite, mit but eingeleitete Satzteil muss nicht unbedingt dastehen, ist aber immer mitgemeint.

Auf used to folgt in der Regel ein INFINITIV

	used to +	INFINITIV		
I	used to	like	her.	She no longer likes her!
You	used to	be	nicer.	Now you are nasty!
He	used to	smoke.		He has given it up.
She	used to	spend	a fortune.	
It	used to	meow	all night.	
We	used to	go	out.	
You	used to	meet	us.	
They	used to	have	a cat.	

Fragen werden mit did gestellt, denn es geht immer um etwas, das in der Vergangenheit so war. Dann wird aus used jedoch use – did drückt ja bereits die Vergangenheit aus.
Did you use to live in Hamburg?   No, I didn't.
Did you use to meet the Scotts?   Yes, I did.
Dasselbe gilt für die Verneinung:
I didn't use to live in Hamburg.
We didn't use to meet the Scotts.

Be / getting used to

Steht vor dem used to das Verb to get in einer beliebigen Zeitform, ändert sich die Bedeutung. Dann heißt es: an etwas gewöhnt sein, sich an etwas gewöhnen etc.

He got used to the sun. Er gewöhnte sich an die Sonne.
She will get used to her work. Sie wird sich an die Arbeit gewöhnen.

Folgt auf das used to ein Verb, steht dieses *immer* mit ing-Endung, denn es handelt sich um ein GERUNDIUM (S. 164), das Verb wird zum SUBSTANTIV = HAUPTWORT.

I am getting used to having rain every day in the mornings.
They got used to breaking the rules.
I am used to doing all the washing up.
You will soon be used to living on your own.

Praxis

It's your turn
Übung 35
Mit USED TO

a. When I was younger, I read a lot. I ＿＿＿＿＿＿ at lot.

b. When we were little, we lived in France. We ＿＿＿＿＿＿

   in France.

c. I (not, can) ＿＿＿＿＿＿ (work) ＿＿＿＿＿＿ long

   hours. (nicht daran gewöhnen können)

d. We (SIMPLE PAST) (get) ＿＿＿＿＿＿ (live) ＿＿＿＿＿＿

   in the city. (uns daran gewöhnen)

e. _____ you _____ like Simply Red when you were

younger?

f. I _____ (get up) _____ at 6 am.

(bin daran gewöhnt)

g. When mother was young, she was pretty. She (be) _____

pretty.

h. When grandma was alive we went there every Sunday.

We (visit) _____ Grandma every Sunday.

Must + must not

Must bedeutet „müssen".
Bei der Verneinung ändert sich jedoch die Bedeutung:
you must   = du musst
you must not   = du darfst nicht   = Verbot
Hinter must oder must not steht immer ein INFINITIV!
I must get some milk for tonight.
You mustn't take food out of the fridge.   Verbot
He must have a haircut.
She must not scream like a madwoman.   Verbot „darfst nicht"
It must be this dress or none.
We mustn't forget to take this bag, too.   „dürfen nicht"
You must arrive before the meeting starts.
They must not throw the rubbish on the floor.

Must gehört zu den MODALVERBEN (S. 176) und hat keine 2. oder 3. FORM wie reguläre Verben. In der Gegenwart (SIMPLE PRESENT) können must und have to alternativ verwendet werden. In der Vergangenheit und Zukunft (SIMPLE PAST und FUTURE) muss man die ERSATZFORM nehmen.

She must/has to go to the doctor.   Gegenwart
She had to go to the doctor.   Vergangenheit
She will have to go to the doctor.   Zukunft

Praxis

It's your turn
Übung 36
SÄTZE mit MUST, MUST NOT, HAD TO bilden

a. Ein Fußballteam darf nicht mehr als elf Spieler auf dem Platz haben.

_____

b. Beim Fußball darf der Ball nicht mit dem Arm gestoppt werden.

_____

c. Die Spieler müssen mit dem Fuß spielen.

_____

d. Ausgetauschte Spieler dürfen nicht wieder eingewechselt werden.

_____

e. Die Regeln müssen eingehalten werden.

_____

f. Die meisten Kinder mussten vor dem Schwimmbad warten.

_____

g. Grundsätzlich dürfen sie nicht ohne die Lehrerin hineingehen.

_____

h. Der Bus musste an der Haltestelle warten, weil die Türen sich nicht schließen ließen.

_____

Gerundium

Das Gerundium ist die Substantivierung des Verbs, das Verb wird also zum Hauptwort. Im Deutschen passiert das, wenn wir ein *das* vor das Verb stellen: lieben – das Lieben, staunen – das Staunen. Im Englischen wird ein Verb mit der ing-Endung zum Substantiv.

PRESENT CONTINUOUS	GERUNDIUM
She is riding.	Riding horses is fun.
We are reading.	He enjoys reading very much.
I am shopping.	We love shopping.

> **!** Die Schwierigkeiten beim Gerundium entstehen durch eine lange Reihe von Ausdrücken und Verben in Verbindung mit oder ohne Präpositionen, auf die ein Gerundium folgen *muss*. Diese feststehenden Ausdrücke muss man lernen, es gibt keine Erklärung dafür. Das Schwierige dabei: Für uns klingen häufig sowohl das Gerundium als auch der Infinitiv richtig:
>
> She admitted having taken the money.   *Richtig*
> She admitted to have taken it.   *Falsch*

Es gibt auch Verben, auf die das Gerundium folgen *kann*, aber nicht muss, d. h. hier haben Sie die Option, auch den Infinitiv zu nutzen.

Verb	GERUNDIUM		INFINITIV
to like	I like swimming.	oder	I like to swim.
to love	I love gardening.	oder	I love to do the garden.
to hate	She hates running.	oder	She hates to run.
to prefer	We prefer driving.	oder	We prefer to drive.
to start	They started walking.	oder	They started to walk.
to begin	She began talking.	oder	She began to talk.

Auf manche Verben wiederum kann *nie* Gerundium folgen, sondern es folgt immer der INFINITIV:

Verb	INFINITIV
to decide	We decided to stay.
to hope	He hopes to find a job very soon.
to learn	She learns to play the guitar.
to plan	They plan to visit her parents next month.
to want	We want to offer you some money.
to offer	We offer to take you up for a while.
to promise	You must promise to keep off that place.
to afford	We cannot afford to buy a house.
to manage	Can you manage to carry that alone?

Ausdrücke, auf die unbedingt das Gerundium folgen muss, lernt man am besten einfach auswendig:

She admitted having taken the money.	zugeben
They are afraid of losing the match.	befürchten
They avoid going on holiday on a Saturday.	vermeiden
She's busy finding the right partner.	beschäftigt sein
I can't help falling in love with you.	nicht anders können
If we carry on sleeping so badly, we may need help.	weitermachen
We considered buying a new house.	in Erwägung ziehen

We are all <u>crazy about</u> going to the cinema.   verrückt sein nach
I will <u>delay</u> telling Max the truth.   verschieben
She <u>denied</u> coming over for dinner.   ablehnen
We <u>dislike</u> reading poems.   mögen nicht
She <u>enjoys</u> riding horses.   genießen
He is <u>famous for</u> singing well.   berühmt sein
I am <u>fed up with</u> being treated as a child.   genug haben von
I am <u>good at</u> painting but <u>bad at</u> lying.   gut/schlecht können
We are not <u>happy about</u> having
    guests on Sunday.   sich freuen über
<u>How about</u> going on holiday together?   wie wäre es
He <u>imagines</u> driving a fast car.   sich vorstellen
Are you <u>interested in</u> writing?   an etwas
        interessiert sein

Mother is <u>keen on</u> learning how to work
    on the computer.   begeistert sein
She <u>misses</u> playing tennis.   vermissen
We will always <u>regret</u> not having bought
    the house.   bedauern
She doesn't want to <u>risk</u> losing her licence.   riskieren
It's <u>no use</u> wasting anymore time here.   keinen Sinn machen
She <u>suggests</u> flying to New York.   vorschlagen

Praxis

It's your turn
Übung 37
GERUNDIUM

a. Ich schlage vor, dass wir uns um 22 Uhr treffen.

_____

b. Sie bestand darauf, selber zum Treffpunkt zu fahren.

_____

c. Wir machen einfach so weiter wie bisher.

_____

d. Es bringt nichts, sich darüber aufzuregen.

_____

e. Wie wäre es, wenn wir zusammen ins Theater gehen?

_____

f. Wir mögen es nicht zu streiten.

_____

g. Sie ist bekannt dafür, gute Bücher zu schreiben.

_____

h. Sie malt sehr gerne.

_____

i. Wir würden sehr gerne nach Australien reisen.

_____

Übung 38
GERUNDIUM oder nicht?

a. She is fed up with him (not to go) _____ to the gym.

b. She decided (to get) _____ a new television.

c. My uncle gave up (to smoke) _____ two years ago.

d. My family wants me (to be) _____ tidy and punctual.

e. I dream about (to have) _____ lots of money.

f. I hope (to see) _____ my friend at the cinema.

g. He would like (to play) _____ chess well.

h. The parents avoid (to leave) _____ their children
   unattended.

Infinitiv

Der Infinitiv ist die GRUNDFORM = 1. FORM jedes Verbs und wird
in den Zeiten bei SIMPLE PRESENT verwendet. Daneben kommt der
Infinitiv auch nach bestimmten Wörtern + Ausdrücken vor. Meistens steht ein to vor dem Infinitiv, aber eben nicht immer:

INFINITIV *ohne* to nach
make/have someone do something
Bedeutung: jemanden dazu bringen, etwas für einen zu tun!

Die Zeitform wird über make/have gebildet.

He made <u>her</u> carry the bags.	SIMPLE PAST
We had <u>a painter</u> do our kitchen.	SIMPLE PAST
She makes <u>him</u> feel rather uncomfortable.	SIMPLE PRESENT
Please have <u>your secretary</u> fax me this information.	IMPERATIV
We have just made <u>him</u> come over.	PRESENT PERFECT

INFINITIV *ohne* to nach
let <u>someone</u> do something
Bedeutung: jemanden etwas machen, tun lassen.
Why don't you let <u>your son</u> decide for himself?
He let <u>his friend</u> drive his motorcycle last week.

INFINITIV *mit* to nach
FRAGEWÖRTERN
I always know <u>who</u> to ask.
Mary told him <u>where</u> to find a good hairdresser.
David can't decide <u>whether</u> to go or not to go to the party.
The teacher told the class <u>when</u> to bring the money.

INFINITIV *mit* to nach
FOR someone
Here is the book <u>for</u> Anna to read.
This is good enough <u>for</u> you to wear, don't you think?
The flat was too small <u>for</u> them to stay for two weeks.
We were waiting <u>for</u> the bus to arrive.

INFINITIV *mit* to nach
ADJECTIVES, ADVERBS, ORDINAL NUMBERS, THE ONLY
It is <u>difficult</u> to learn Chinese.
He said he wasn't very <u>likely</u> to pass the exam.
The <u>most popular</u> star to sing at the concert was Katy Perry.

I was the <u>first</u> to get an award.
Tom was <u>the only</u> boy to enter the competition.

INFINITIV *mit* to nach
SOMEBODY, ANYBODY
We desperately need <u>someone</u> to help us with the garden.
He doesn't know <u>anybody</u> to talk to when he has a problem.

> **!** Die genannten Beispiele zeigen, wann ein Infinitiv verwendet
> werden *kann*, das bedeutet nicht, dass hinter diesen Wörtern
> immer ein Infinitiv steht!

Adjektive

Adjektive beschreiben eine Sache oder eine Person genauer: *Wie* ist
etwas oder jemand (nett, frech, traurig, hübsch, schlecht etc.)
Wie jemand *ist*, erfordert zusätzlich das Verb SEIN = to be.
Bei Adjektiven wird daher meistens eine Form von to be verwendet.
The girl is nice. This is a nice girl.
The boy is nasty. It's a nasty boy.
I am sad. I am a sad person.
The show will be good.
This is going to be a wonderful weekend.
It has been amazing.
The exam was bad.

> **!** Das bringt soweit keine Schwierigkeiten mit sich. Anders ist das
> beim Steigern und Vergleichen!

Steigern + vergleichen

Adjektive können gesteigert werden, aus *nett* wird *netter,* bzw. *am nettesten*. Damit lassen sich Dinge und Personen vergleichen. Die Steigerung von Adjektiven erfolgt in drei Schritten: Grundform (Adjektiv), 1. Steigerungsform (Komparativ) und 2. Steigerungsform (Superlativ).

Deutsch

SCHRITT 1	SCHRITT 2	SCHRITT 3
nett	netter	am nettesten
frech	frecher	am frechsten
traurig	trauriger	am traurigsten

Englisch

1. Einsilbige Adjektive und zweisilbige Adjektive, die auf -y, -ow und -le enden:

SCHRITT 1	SCHRITT 2 Endung -er	SCHRITT 3 Endung -est	
nice	nicer	nicest	
small	smaller	smallest	
cheeky	cheekier	cheekiest	y = ie
nasty	nastier	nastiest	y = ie
shallow	shallower	shallowest	
simple	simpler	simplest	

2. Bei zwei- und mehrsilbigen Adjektiven funktionieren die Endungen nicht, hier werden beim Komparativ more und beim Superlativ (the) most vorangestellt:

SCHRITT 1	SCHRITT 2	SCHRITT 3
beautiful	more beautiful	most beautiful
extraordinary	more extraordinary	most extraordinary
difficult	more difficult	most difficult
magnificent	more magnificent	most magnificent

AUSNAHMEN: unregelmässig gesteigerte Adjektive

SCHRITT 1	SCHRITT 2	SCHRITT 3
bad	worse	worst
good	better	best
little	less	least
much	more	most
many	more	most

Bigger than

Wenn man bei Vergleichen den Komparativ benutzt, wird than „als" verwendet.

The new boat is bigger than the old one.	größer als
Your backpack is more comfortable than mine.	bequemer als
His shoes are cooler than hers.	cooler als

Will man eine Aussage noch verstärken, kann much benutzt werden:
This jacket is <u>much</u> more comfortable than that one.

viel bequemer als

These glasses are <u>much</u> cooler than those yellow ones.

viel cooler als

> **!** one/s dient im Englischen als Platzhalter. In Sätzen mit Vergleichen wird es oft verwendet, muss aber nicht, es sei denn, nach that, those etc. steht noch ein Adjektiv: those small ones.

As much as

Wenn man bei Vergleichen Gleichheit ausdrücken will, dann wird die Grundform benutzt und as … as „(genau)so … wie" benötigt:
This booklet is as good as the other one, believe me.
She is as helpful as an angel.
This year she is not doing as well as she did last year.
Can the Jaguar drive as fast as the MG?
She is as bright as her sister.

Adverbien

Adverbien beschreiben vor allem Verben genauer: *Wie* ein Ding oder eine Person etwas tut. Hierfür wird dem englischen Adjektiv die Endung -ly angehängt. Im Deutschen werden unverändert die Adjektivformen verwendet, deshalb sind die Adverbien in der Anwendung im Englischen ungewohnt:

Das Kleid *ist* schön.   The dress is beautiful.   Adjektiv
Das Mädchen *spielt* schön.   The girl plays beautifully.   Adverb

Adverbien =

Adjektiv + ly

Adverbien können am SATZANFANG, in der SATZMITTE oder am SATZENDE stehen:

Diabolically he smiles at her.
The stock market is becoming increasingly worried about China.
He sings beautifully.
The cat meows loudly.

Sie dürfen jedoch nicht zwischen Verb + Objekt stehen:

She plays the piano beautifully.   Richtig
She plays beautifully the piano.   Falsch

Unregelmässige Adverbien

Adjektiv	Adverb
good	well
fast	fast

hard	hard	(Achtung: hardly = kaum)
He plays hard.	spielt angestrengt	Aber: He hardly plays.
		(kaum/fast nie)

This car drives well.	fährt gut
The car drives fast.	fährt schnell

Endet ein Adjektiv auf -ly, wird das Adverb mit Hilfe dieser Phrase gebildet:

silly	in a silly way
friendly	in a friendly way

! Adverbien beschreiben nicht nur Verben näher, sondern auch andere Adverbien, Adjektive oder ganze Sätze.

They worked extremely slowly.	Adverb
We found a new flat really fast.	Adjektiv
Unfortunately, there was nothing left when they arrived.	
	ganzer Satz

! Bei Verben der Sinneswahrnehmung, eines Zustands oder einer Eigenschaft wird häufig das Adjektiv verwendet, denn diese Verben können durch to be ersetzt werden (nach to be steht ein Adjektiv).

This cake tastes delicious.	meint: This cake is delicious.
The flowers smell very nice.	meint: The flowers are very nice.

Vergleiche:

Peter looks good.	Peter looks well.
Er sieht gut aus.	Er sieht gesund aus.

Praxis

It's your turn
Übung 39
ADJEKTIVE + ADVERBIEN

a. In the afternoon they (kurz) _____ had a meeting with
the board.

b. They started to climb a (hoch) _____ mountain.

c. The meeting was (interessanter) _____ than they had
thought.

d. This dish smells (lecker) _____.

e. This is a (schön geschnitten) _____ cut dress.

f. We met the (größten) _____ of all artists.

g. This house is (genauso gut wie) _____ the other one.

h. This hotel has been (sehr empfohlen) _____ in the
guide.

Übung 40
ADJEKTIVE + ADVERBIEN

a. She was (nicht schnell genug) _____ sending
the mail.

b. He did his homework (viel besser) _____ this time.

c. A year ago we didn't speak English (gut) _____

d. The two kids crossed the road (vorsichtig) _____

e. The manager shouted (wütend) _____

f. We spent a (günstig) _____ holiday.

g. The hotel on the beach is (viel teurer) _____
than ours.

h. He played (glücklich) _____ on his piano.

Modalverben

Modalverben wie can, should, must beschreiben Wünsche, Möglichkeiten und Zwänge. Sie haben jedoch keine 2. und 3. Form wie reguläre Verben. Einige Modalverben sind wenig bekannt, andere werfen Fragen auf. Weniger bekannt sind die Ersatzformen der Modalverben, denn werden can, should, must in anderen Zeiten als SIMPLE PRESENT verwendet, müssen oft die Ersatzformen herangezogen werden.

> **!** Generell gilt:
> Auf ein Modalverb folgt immer ein Infinitiv.

Can = be able to (Ersatzform)

Mit can wird um Erlaubnis gefragt und ausgedrückt, ob jemand etwas kann, physisch oder geistig. Can kann im SIMPLE PAST mit could gebildet werden, für andere Zeiten wird be able to zwingend benötigt:

Can I open the window please, it's much
   too warm in here.   Erlaubnis
I don't know if she can speak Chinese.   Können
I didn't know if she was able to/could
   speak Chinese.   SIMPLE PAST
I am sure she can't speak Japanese, though.   Verneinung
She has never been able to learn
   a foreign language.   PRESENT PEFECT
SHE wasn't able to/couldn't see properly.   SIMPLE PAST
They will be able to move together now.   WILL FUTURE

Could

Could bedeutet „könnte/konnte". Es wird damit eine Möglichkeit ausgedrückt, dient als Höflichkeitsform und kommt vor als Vergangenheitsform SIMPLE PAST von can:

I guess I could go to evening classes.   Möglichkeit
Could you please turn the radio down a bit?   Höflichkeit
When she was younger, she couldn't
   speak Chinese.   SIMPLE PAST
We couldn't have been happier.   SIMPLE PAST
                                         Verneinung

May = be allowed to (Ersatzform)

May fragt um Erlaubnis „dürfen" und ist etwas förmlicher als can. May drückt auch aus, dass etwas sein könnte, also eine Möglichkeit. Dieses Modalverb kommt nicht in der Vergangenheit vor, denn es bezieht sich immer auf etwas in der Gegenwart oder Zukunft. Für die Bildung aller Zeiten außer Gegenwart wird die Ersatzform be allowed to verwendet:

May I open the door for you?   förmlich
This call may be for me.   Möglichkeit
Or this may not be for us.   Verneinung
Last year we were allowed to go to the prom.   SIMPLE PAST
Next year, we will not be allowed to go there. WILL FUTURE

Might

Might drückt immer aus, dass etwas sein könnte, also eine Möglichkeit. Auch might kommt nicht in der Vergangenheit vor, denn es bezieht sich immer auf etwas in der Zukunft:

The weather forecast says it might rain later.	Möglichkeit
I might not feel well enough to go to the interview.	Verneinung

Must = have to (Ersatzform)

Must heißt „müssen", ist also ein Befehl oder Zwang. Um Vergangenheit oder Zukunft bilden zu können, wird have to verwendet. Wird must verneint, erhält es eine andere Bedeutung: nicht dürfen = Verbot (S. 162):

We must book our journey before it's fully booked.	Zwang
Last year we had to sell our car.	SIMPLE PAST
Our neighbours didn't have to sell theirs though.	SIMPLE PAST
They will have to find a new place soon.	WILL FUTURE

Need to = have to (Ersatzform)

Need to bedeutet „brauchen/müssen", ist aber nicht so stark wie der Befehl must. Wie bei must gibt es die Ersatzform have to, aber need to funktioniert auch im SIMPLE PRESENT + SIMPLE PAST:

I need to get a present for Peter this week.	brauchen
We need to talk about the further steps for the project.	Notwendigkeit
Does my secretary have to/need to attend?	FRAGE
No, she doesn't have to/need to be there.	SIMPLE PRESENT Verneinung
We needed to get some food urgently.	SIMPLE PAST

Need not (be)

Needn't = need not bedeutet „nicht brauchen/nicht müssen" und wird häufig auch als PASSIV (S. 187) verwendet:

It need not be emphasized that it is a priority project.   Passiv

If I go jogging today I need not go swimming
    on Thursday.   Aktiv

Ought to / shall / should = be supposed to / be expected to (Ersatzformen)

Alle drei Formen bedeuten „sollen/sollten". Es ist in der Regel eine Erwartung von außen vorhanden. Ought to impliziert eher eine eigene moralische Verpflichtung. Es existieren die Ersatzformen be supposed to und be expected to:

What shall we do with the broken chair?   sollen
I should take the waste outside.   Erwartung von außen
We ought to ask your father about it.   sollten (moralisch)
I remember you were supposed to be   SIMPLE PAST
    back by 11 pm.   Ersatzform
I was expected to care for my parents.   SIMPLE PAST
                                                Ersatzform

Praxis

It's your turn
Übung 41
SÄTZE MIT MODALVERBEN BILDEN

a. Sie musste länger bleiben.

_____

b. Durftest du gestern ins Kino gehen?

_____

c. Er darf jetzt nicht einschlafen.

_____

d. Er sollte nicht alles aufessen.

_____

e. Es könnte sein, dass wir heute später anfangen.

_____

f. Ihr braucht nicht auf uns zu warten.

_____

g. Das solltet ihr nicht verpassen.

_____

h. Das würden wir sehr gerne mit euch ansehen.

_____

Übung 42
ERSATZFORMEN von MODALVERBEN einsetzen

a. We should win the game. = We _____ win the game.

b. She could swim very fast. = She _____ swim very fast.

c. They may stay up late tonight. = They _____ stay up late.

d. They need not take the car. = They _____ take the car.

e. We must finish the project soon. = We _____ finish soon.

f. You must not drive more than 60 miles per hour. = You

_____ drive more than 60 miles per hour.

g. We should not drink Coke every day. = We _____

drink Coke every day.

h. The children shall bring their lunch. = They _____

_____ bring their lunch.

Übung 43
IN VERGANGENHEIT (SIMPLE PAST) SETZEN

a. Thomas <u>must</u> tidy his office because he <u>cannot</u> find anything.

_____

b. His mother <u>tells</u> him he <u>should be</u> tidier.

_____

c. You <u>must not</u> keep us waiting.

_____

d. If the work <u>is</u> not good enough, he <u>need not</u> panic.

_____

e. The lady <u>can</u> help in the kindergarten.

_____

Question tags

Question tags sind Frageanhängsel und werden vor allem in der gesprochenen Sprache verwendet, nämlich immer dann, wenn der Sprecher eine Bestätigung auf seine Aussage einholen will, vergleichbar dem deutschen „… nicht wahr? … oder etwa nicht?". Geschrieben sieht man sie eher selten. Wichtig ist: Question tags greifen immer die jeweils verwendete Zeit in entgegengesetzter Form auf:
Ist die Aussage positiv: QUESTION TAG negativ.
Ist die Aussage negativ: QUESTION TAG positiv.
Die Sätze werden immer so gebildet, wie dies die verwendete Zeit erfordert:

	QUESTION TAG
This is a nice hat,	isn't it?
Your son plays football,	doesn't he?
I am late,	am I not?
We are having fun,	aren't we?
You haven't cooked,	have you?
She has made a mistake,	hasn't she?
They didn't win,	did they?
We met them there,	didn't we?
We could join them,	couldn't we?
She can't play tennis,	can she?
They might be tired,	might they not?
He will be 17 today,	won't he?
They had lost,	hadn't they?
They were losing,	weren't they?
We are going to buy a pool,	aren't we?

Achtung:

Let's get ice-cream,	shall we?
Open the window,	will you?

Relativsätze who + which

Who, which, that leiten RELATIVSÄTZE = RELATIVE CLAUSES ein. Das sind Nebensätze, die eine Sache oder Person im Hauptsatz genauer bestimmen.

The boy, who worked at the café, was very nice.
We drove through Oxford Street, which took a lot of time.
The bus that broke down had to be towed by a special lorry.

who
für
Personen

which
für
Dinge

that
für Personen
& Dinge

! Wichtig: Who wird nur bei Personen und which nur bei Dingen verwendet. Manchmal kann that verwendet werden, jedoch nicht immer (siehe nachfolgende Seiten). Als Hilfestellung lässt sich aber sagen: Gewöhnen Sie sich an, *immer* who für PERSONEN und which für DINGE zu benutzen, dann können Sie weniger falsch machen.

MIT oder OHNE who oder which
Die Regeln zu RELATIVSÄTZEN sind nicht ganz einfach. Es geht dabei um die Frage, in welchen Fällen die Relativpronomen weggelassen werden können und in welchen Fällen sie unbedingt benutzt werden müssen. Vereinfacht ausgedrückt lässt sich zusammenfassen:

1. Steht hinter who/that oder which/that nicht direkt ein VERB – sondern dann meistens eine Person –, kann das Pronomen weggelassen werden.
The girl (who/that) we met on holiday is from Holland.
The bag (which/that) I shall take with me is next to the door.
I don't like the trousers (which/that) my mother bought me.

2. Steht direkt hinter who/that oder which/that ein VERB, muss das Pronomen verwendet werden!
We threw away everything which/that was left.
A pilot is someone who/that flies a plane.
There was nobody at the party who/that wore a suit.

Die unter 1. und 2. genannten Sätze sind Beispiele für sogenannte DEFINING RELATIVE CLAUSES (BESTIMMENDER RELATIVSATZ): Der Relativsatz bestimmt das Wort genauer, auf das er sich bezieht – ohne diesen Zusatz hätte der Satz eine andere Bedeutung. Vergleichen Sie: We threw away everything. – We threw away everything which was left.
Daneben gibt es die NON-DEFINING RELATIVE CLAUSE (NICHT BESTIMMENDER RELATIVSATZ): Dieser Relativsatz enthält lediglich eine Zusatzinformation, ohne die der Rest des Satzes sich nicht verändert – und diese wird mit Komma abgegrenzt. Diese Sätze finden sich eher in formellem Englisch. Für Schüler, die vor allem Sprechen wollen, ist das daher nicht vorrangig. Es soll hier aber der grammatikalischen Vollständigkeit halber erwähnt werden.

Teil Drei – Damit wird es komplett

3. Steht ein Relativsatz mit Komma, muss who oder which verwendet werden, aber that kann *nicht* verwendet werden!
Yesterday we went to the zoo, which was very nice.
The film star, who I saw in many films, is Tom Cruise.
John, who we met yesterday, has his own company.
Im Sprachbebrauch wird das eher so ausgedrückt: John has his own company and we met him yesterday.

TIPP: Die Regeln zur korrekten Anwendung der Relativpronomen sind kompliziert, daher gilt: Für den mündlichen Sprachgebrauch sind sie nicht vorrangig, da kommt es vor allem darauf an, für Personen nicht which und für Dinge nicht who zu verwenden!

Who / which in a nutshell

who für PERSONEN

which für DINGE

that für PERSONEN und DINGE
(wenn kein Komma steht)

BEI UNSICHERHEIT: lieber who
oder which verwenden!

Whose + whom

Weitere Einleitungen für Relativsätze sind whose und whom. Whose „dessen/deren" steht für eine ZUGEHÖRIGKEIT zu Personen, Tieren oder Dingen. In Fragen heißt whose „wessen". Whom „dem/den, die/der" wird verwendet, wenn das Pronomen die Funktion eines Objekts übernimmt.
The man, whose daughter is in my class, is sitting over there.
The cat, whose tail is black and white, has come back.

Whose iPad is this?
She met John, whom she hadn't seen for ages.
We were invited by the couple whom we had met on holiday.

> ❗ Umgangssprachlich wird hier häufig auch who verwendet, was auch OK ist.

When + where + why

Auch when, where und why können Einleitungen zu Nebensätzen sein.

This is the house where we used to live.
    auch: … in which we used to live.
The 24th of October is the day when we met.
    auch: … on which we met.
This is the reason why I am not coming.
    auch: … for which I am not coming.

Praxis

It's your turn
Übung 44
WHO, WHICH, THAT oder OHNE?

a. The book _____ I am reading, is about World War II.

b. This is the flat _____ we looked at last month.

c. Peter, _____ comes round every night, is a lonely guy.

d. This is Mary _____ lives next door.

e. Mary's two dogs, _____ are black, can play in the garden.

f. Tamara's cats, _____ can play outside, are black and white.

g. A pickpocket is someone _____ steals purses and money.

h. A tiger is an animal _____ lives in Asia.

Übung 45
SÄTZE VERBINDEN MIT WHO, WHOM, WHOSE oder WHICH

a. She is a hairdresser. She has no job at the moment.

b. Tim is a musician. I saw him at a festival.

c. Dad got the letter. I sent it from Spain last week.

d. This is the exam. I find it very difficult.

e. This is our neighbour. His wife ran off.

f. Thomas lives next door. He won the lottery.

g. They came to my party. It was very kind of them.

h. The meal was delicious. We enjoyed it.

Passiv

Passiv kommt im Sprachgebrauch sehr oft vor. PASSIV bedeutet, dass eine Person oder eine Sache etwas nicht selbst tut, sondern etwas mit ihm oder ihr passiert. Mein Vater fährt zur Arbeit = aktiv. Aber: Mein Vater wird zur Arbeit gefahren = passiv.

My father built this house.   aktiv
This house was built in 1934 (by my grand-father).   passiv

The city council closed the school.   aktiv
The school was closed last year.   passiv

I usually wake up at 7 am.   aktiv
I usually am woken up at 7 am.   passiv
Vergleiche: My mom wakes me up.   aktiv

> ❗ Passiv wird von vielen Lernenden ganz automatisch richtig ver-
> wendet, aber bei Nachfragen, was Passiv sei, fehlen oft Antwor-
> ten. Für gute und sichere Sprachkenntnisse ist es hilfreich zu
> wissen, was Passiv bedeutet und wie man es bildet.

Passiv bilden

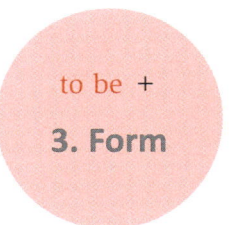

to be +

3. Form

Passiv wird im Englischen *immer* aus einer Form von to be (entsprechend der benutzten Zeit) + der 3. FORM des Verbs gebildet.

Passiv gibt es in allen Zeiten:

	to be	3. FORM
SIMPLE PRESENT	is	stolen
PRESENT CONTINUOUS	is being	stolen
PRESENT PERFECT	has been	stolen
SIMPLE PAST	was	stolen

PAST CONTINUOUS	was being	stolen
PAST PERFECT	had been	stolen
FUTURE WILL	will be	stolen
FUTURE GOING TO	is going to be	stolen
FUTURE CONTINUOUS	is being	stolen
FUTURE SIMPLE PRESENT	is	stolen
CONDITIONAL I	will be	stolen
CONDITIONAL II	would be	stolen
CONDITIONAL III	would have been	stolen

AUSSAGEN, FRAGEN + VERNEINUNGEN werden entsprechend der Regeln der jeweiligen Zeit gebildet:

I thought the work had been <u>done</u> better.

Wasn't the cake <u>brought</u> to the wedding by the bakery?

Would the ring have been <u>stolen</u> if we had put it in the safe, do you think?

The tree is being <u>taken</u> down today, what a shame.

Ms Fuchs said the letter had been <u>sent</u> by her.

The game is going to be <u>called</u> off due to the weather.

Susan is <u>taken</u> to tennis every week.

The baby was <u>comforted</u> by its mother.

This hasn't been <u>done</u> very carefully, has it?

The patient must be <u>taken</u> to hospital.

The paper shouldn't been <u>thrown</u> in the non-recyclable waste.

Praxis

It's your turn
Übung 46
SÄTZE BILDEN im PASSIV

a. Der Politiker wurde zum Interview gebeten.

_____

b. Das Projekt kann doch noch finanziert werden.

_____

c. Der neue Roman wird von den Kritikern gelobt.

_____

d. Die Bauarbeiten können am Samstag beendet werden.

_____

e. Die Batterie muss ersetzt werden.

_____

f. Die gesamte Prüfung muss wiederholt werden.

_____

g. Der Manager hätte über das Problem informiert sein sollen.

_____

h. Wir sind alle zu Marias Party eingeladen.

_____

Übung 47
PASSIVSÄTZE BILDEN in richtiger ZEIT

a. my car / to break into (PRESENT PERFECT)

_____

b. the group / to see in the park (SIMPLE PAST)

_____

c. curtain / to hang up at the weekend (GOING TO FUTURE)

_____

d. inline skates / to use before (PAST PERFECT)

_____

e. the museum / to close (CONDITIONAL I)

_____

f. Susan / to tell to give up smoking (SIMPLE PAST)

_____

g. table / to lay (WILL FUTURE)

_____

h. book / to give to me (PRESENT PERFECT)

_____

Übung 48
SÄTZE BILDEN im AKTIV und PASSIV

a. Weintrauben wachsen/werden angebaut in Kalifornien.

AKTIV   _____

PASSIV   _____

b. Das Kind wäscht sich/wird gewaschen.

AKTIV   _____

PASSIV   _____

c. Die Gruppe gibt auf/wird aufgegeben.

AKTIV   _____

PASSIV   _____

d. Der kleine Junge haut den großen/wird vom großen Jungen gehauen.

AKTIV   _____

PASSIV   _____

e. Die Polizei sah den Dieb/wurde vom Dieb gesehen.

AKTIV   _____

PASSIV   _____

Präpositionen

Präpositionen sind ein wichtiges Thema für Englischlernende. Hier werden gängige und wichtige Präpositionen aufgelistet – was nicht heißt, dass nicht noch weitere existieren. Besonders gut einprägen sollte man sich die Präpositionen der ZEIT und des ORTES, denn diese kommen immer wieder vor und werden leicht durcheinandergeworfen.

Warum eine Präposition an dieser oder jener Stelle stehen muss, lässt sich oft nicht erklären. Präpositionen sind wie Vokabeln, die man lernt.

Präpositionen der **Zeit**

TAGESZEITEN UND DATEN mit on, in, at

Warum für verschiedene Zeiten verschiedene Präpositionen benutzt werden, weiß man nicht. Also einfach merken! So heißt es richtig:

On

Tage, Feiertage

We'll meet on Monday or on Tuesday, if you like.

On Christmas day, our family eats turkey.

On Easter Sunday, we visit friends.

In

Tageszeiten, Jahreszeiten, Jahreszahlen, in einem Tag, einer Woche, Monate

I do my shopping in the morning.

In the evenings, the meetings start at 20 hours.

In winter, precisely in March, we go skiing.

In 2013 they broke into our house.

In three month time we move house.

At

Mittags, nachts, Uhrzeiten, am Wochenende, zur Osterzeit, zur Weihnachtszeit

I have a nap at lunchtime.
I usually don`t have to get up at night.
School starts at 9 o'clock on time.
At the weekend we usually visit my parents.
Do we meet at Easter?
What do you do at Christmas?

In a nutshell

on Monday & Easter Sunday
in the evening & the morning
in March, spring, winter & 1934
in 2012 & an hour
in the end & the beginning
at 8 o'clock & half past eight
at midday, lunchtime & night
at the weekend

Ago, before, to, past, until, by

Ago

Mit Zeitpunkt in der Vergangenheit

I had my last pay-rise two years ago.
We got married ten years ago.

Before

Vor einem Zeitpunkt

The dog was already here before I met my husband.
You must be home before midnight.

To + past

Für Uhrzeiten vor & nach
What time is it? It's ten to six.
You have to leave at ten past six!

From … to + until/till

Von … bis
School is from Monday to Friday.
They have lessons until/till half past eleven every day.

By

Bis dahin ist etwas passiert, Frist
The document needs to be ready by Friday morning at the latest.
By ten o'clock, she was feeling rather ill.

Präpositionen des **Ortes**, **Position** und **Richtung**

In

Räumlich drinnen, in einem Raum,
einem Fahrzeug, aber auch innerhalb
einer Stadt, auf der Welt und auf dem Foto,
in dem Buch, auf der Straße, auf einer Insel:
in a room, in the kitchen, in the car, in London, in Paris, in town, in
the world, in the picture, in the book, in the street, in the Maldives

At

Räumlich nahe dran, in der Nähe von,
am Tisch, bei einem Ereignis, an einem bestimmten Ort:
at the door, at the table, at a party, at a meeting, at the station, at
school, at work, at home, at the cinema

On + onto

Räumlich auf etwas (einem Untergrund),
aber auch an der Wand, rechts, links, auf
Etagen, in öffentlichen Verkehrsmitteln, im
Fernsehen, Radio, Internet, an einem Fluss:
onto: auf etwas hinauf (-legen oder -springen):

on the table, on the floor, on the wall, on the left, on the right, on
the second floor, on the bus, on the plane, on the tube, on television,
on the radio, on the internet, Düsseldorf is on the Rhine, onto the
table, onto the sofa

By + next to

Räumlich (da)neben:
by the window, by the table, next to
the sofa, next to me

Under + below

Bedeuten beide „unter/unterhalb" von
etwas, under kommt häufiger vor, below
bedeutet lower than und passt nicht
immer, daher im Zweifel under verwenden.
Under auch: unter neuer Führung.
We are sitting under a tree.
Draw a line under/below each word.
Temperatures are below average.
The company is under a new management.

Over + above

Bedeuten beide „über", wobei mit over
eher eine Bewegung einhergeht, bei above
ist etwas platziert. Die Redewendung over
and above bedeutet übrigens
„zusätzlich/darüber hinaus":

They climbed over the fence.
He leaned over to see what she was doing.
Could you come over please, I've got something for you.
The lamp hangs above the table.
You can use my email, as shown above.
Over and above the alternative is not to leave.

Across + through

Bedeuten „hinüber" und „durch" –
bei across geht es in der Regel nicht
durch einen Tunnel oder Wald (etwas
bedecktes), sondern über eine Straße,
eine Brücke, through dagegen geht durch einen Raum, Tunnel:
They walked across the bridge.
They had to swim across the river.
We made our way through the forest.
I ran through the crowd.

To + into

Bedeuten „zu/nach" und „hinein",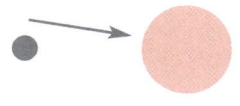
also ich gehe zum Friseur, zum Shop,
bin ich dort angekommen, gehe ich
hinein, beide beinhalten also eine
Richtung, ein Ziel:
The class is driving to London by bus.
Are you walking to the Smiths?
No, I am on my way to the hair-dresser.
He arrived and went into the shop straight away.
They jumped into the pool.

Towards

Towards bedeutet „in Richtung". Man kann in eine Richtung gehen, dorthin zeigen, sich orientieren. Wenn man Richtung Bahnhof geht, heißt es ja nicht, dass man zum Bahnhof geht!
They walked towards the river.
Now we must turn towards the tower, don't we?

Up + down

Bedeuten „hinauf/rauf" und „hinunter/runter". To feel down bedeuten außerdem „betrübt/traurig":
The children noisily ran up and down the stairs.
Does this lift go up?
Who lives downstairs?
She felt very down.

Between

„Zwischen" etwas oder jemandem:
They shared the apple between them.
The teacher put a girl between two boys.

Weitere Präpositionen

From, of, for

Sehr häufig werden of und from verwechselt, wenn man sagen will: Das ist das Haus *von* meinen Eltern. Viele übersetzen hier „von" wörtlich mit from, was aber falsch ist, denn es muss heißen:
This is the house of my uncle. = This is my uncle's house.
Daher: Immer wenn man den Satz auch mit 's bilden könnte: of verwenden!

From

Impliziert im Englischen eine Bewegung (von mir zu dir), ein Weitergeben oder ein Voranschreiten der Zeit:

I got this present from my sister.	hat sie mir gegeben
We bought this car from the garage.	in der Werkstatt gekauft
The fair is from Friday till Sunday.	Zeitspanne von bis

Of

Bezeichnet dagegen die Zugehörigkeit zu etwas oder einer Person und kommt häufiger vor:

This is the cat of my neighbour.	gehört dem Nachbarn
This is a CD of Meatloaf.	von Meatloaf
This meat is of good quality.	hat eine gute Qualität
This is a page of the book of my friend.	im Buch meines Freundes
The ring is made of gold.	aus Gold

For

Hat viele Bedeutungen, die man wie eigenständige Redewendungen lernen sollte:

This pullover is for you.	für dich
Has anybody asked for me?	nach mir gefragt
We left for a trip to France.	zu einem Ausflug
They decided to go for a walk.	spazieren gehen
Let's cook, for a change.	zur Abwechslung
These are our products for example.	zum Beispiel
The house is for sale	zum Verkauf
For this reason I like her.	aus diesem Grund
What are we having for lunch.	zum Mittagessen

By, on, in, off, out of

By

Von jemandem gemacht, pro Stunde/Woche:

This is a book by Stephen King.	von Stephen King
This was broken by the cat.	von der Katze
We are paid by the hour.	pro Stunde

On

Zu Fuß, auf dem Rücken eines Pferdes, im Urlaub, pünktlich, zu einem Anlass:

You can either travel on foot,	zu Fuß
or on horseback.	reiten
We are on holiday.	im Urlaub
He arrived on time.	pünktlich
I want to thank you on this occasion.	zu diesem Anlass

In

Viele Bedeutungen, die man lernen muss wie Vokabeln:

in addition to	zusätzlich
in case of an emergency	im Notfall
in fact	tatsächlich
in common	etwas gemeinsam haben
in general	im Allgemeinen
in love	verliebt
in my opinion	meiner Meinung nach
in particular	besonders
in principle	prinzipiell
in the end	schließlich
in the long run	auf Dauer
in time	rechtzeitig

Off

Ein öffentliches Verkehrsmittel verlassen:
to get off a plane, off a train, off an underground

Out of

Aus dem Auto/Taxi steigen, herauskommen:
to get out of the car, out of the taxi, out of a storm

After, at, about, past, among

After

Hinterher, letztendlich, nach allem:
The police ran after the thief.
After all, you are older than your brother.
After all this, I cannot trust you anymore.

At

Im Alter von, in regelmäßigem Abstand:
She did her exam at 23.
She got a car at 18.
at regular intervals

About

Über etwas sprechen, von etwas handeln:
We are talking about something or someone.
This book is about the World War II.

Past

Vorbei an:
Walk past the hairdresser before you turn left.
We walked past the museum on our way to the restaurant.

Among

Unter, innerhalb einer Gruppe (nicht neben zwei):

There was no doctor among the passengers.

There were 10,000 in the arena and I was among them.

Phrasal verbs

PHRASAL VERBS sind Verben mit angehängter Präposition. Man muss sie lernen wie Vokabeln:

to agree with	einverstanden sein
to be in	da (zuhause) sein
to break away/free	sich davonmachen, losreißen
to break down	liegen bleiben
to break up	sich trennen
to bring up	erziehen (Kinder), erwähnen (Thema)
to call off	absagen, abblasen
to calm down	sich, jemanden beruhigen
to carry on	weitermachen
to cut out	aufhören, ausschneiden
to do without	entbehren, verzichten
to drop in	kurz vorbeischauen
to drop off	absetzen, vorbeibringen
to ease off	sich beruhigen, entspannen
to end up	enden
to fall through	ins Wasser fallen
to figure out	herausfinden, verstehen
to fill out	ausfüllen (Formular)
to focus on	sich konzentrieren auf
to get along with	sich verstehen mit, zurechtkommen
to get at	auf etwas hinauswollen (Thema)
to get into	angenommen werden
to get on with	weitermachen mit, sich mit jmd. verstehen

to give up	aufgeben
to go through	durchsuchen, durchkommen, durchstehen, proben
to hand out	verteilen, aushändigen
to hang up	auflegen
to hold on	warten
to hurry up	sich beeilen
to insist on	auf etwas bestehen
to keep at	dabeibleiben, weitermachen
to keep off	nicht betreten
to keep out	draußen bleiben, sich raushalten
to knock off	aufhören mit
to lead up to	hinführen zu, hinauswollen auf
to let down	im Stich lassen
to let in	hereinlassen
to lie down	(sich) hinlegen
to light up	aufleuchten, erleuchten
to line up	sich anstellen
to live up to	etwas/jmd. gerecht werden
to look back on	zurückschauen
to look for	suchen
to look after	aufpassen auf
to make out	entziffern, verstehen
to make up	erfinden, nachholen, wiedergutmachen
to mess up	schmutzig, unordentlich machen
to move on	übergehen zu, weitermachen mit
to open up	(sich) öffnen
to pass away	sterben
to pay off	sich auszahlen, bezahlt machen
to pick up	hochheben, abholen, wachsen, aufschnappen
to point out	aufzeigen, darlegen
to pop up	auftauchen
to pull in(to)	hineinfahren, parken

to pull up	heraufziehen
to put on	anziehen, jemanden auf den Arm nehmen
to put off	(zeitlich) verschieben
to put together	zusammenstellen
to rattle off	herunterleiern
to read over	durchlesen
to rely on	sich auf etwas/jemanden verlassen
to run away	weglaufen
to run off with	abhauen mit
to run out of	nicht mehr da haben
to rush in(to)	hereinstürzen, -stürmen
to save up	ansparen
to see through	durchschauen, betreuen
to settle down	sich niederlassen, sich beruhigen
to show off	angeben, prahlen
to sign up for	sich anmelden
to sit in on	dabei sein
to sit out	aussetzen
to sleep in	ausschlafen
to slim down	abnehmen
to slit up	einen Fehler machen
to smash into	einschlagen, hineinfahren in
to sober up	ausnüchtern
to sort itself out	sich einpendeln
to speak up	lauter sprechen
to speak up for	sich einsetzen für
to spread out	(sich) ausbreiten
to stand around	herumstehen
to stand by	sich bereithalten, warten
to stand in (for)	einspringen
to stay over	übernachten
to stick together	zusammenhalten
to stop by	vorbeischauen

to stop over	übernachten
to sum up	zusammenfassen
to switch on/off	an/ausschalten
to take away	mitnehmen, wegnehmen
to take apart	auseinandernehmen, -bauen
to take over	übernehmen (Posten, Macht)
to talk back (to)	widersprechen
to talk over	besprechen
to team up (with)	sich zusammentun, arbeiten
to tell off	ausschimpfen
to tell on	melden, verraten
to think through	gründlich durchdenken
to throw up	sich übergeben
to try out	ausprobieren
to turn in	ins Bett gehen, einbiegen
to turn up	hochkrempeln, passieren, auftauchen
to use up	aufbrauchen
to walk off	abhauen

PHRASAL VERBS können in jeder Grammatikzeit verwendet werden. Dabei verändert sich das Verb entsprechend. Die Präposition bleibt unverändert.

Beispiel: to walk off/out + to let in

Every night David lets the cat in before he goes to bed.	SIMPLE PRESENT
What are you doing? I am letting the visitors in.	PRESENT CONTINUOUS
Her husband walked off/out three years ago.	SIMPLE PAST
The police found out he had let the thief in.	PAST PERFECT
If you don't treat him better, he will walk off/out one day!	WILL FUTURE

Praxis

It's your turn
Übung 49
PRÄPOSITIONEN EINSETZEN

a. You must check the petrol _____ regular intervals.

b. You can get a person to do it for you. _____ all, you are the boss.

c. _____ this occasion I want to express my thanks.

d. _____ the end nothing was how we had expected it.

e. _____ Christmas day our family eat turkey.

f. _____ the end of the week, you must have finished the project.

g. We wanted to get out _____ a big storm.

h. His contract will be confirmed _____ February.

i. There's an excellent hairdresser _____ the end of the street.

j. There were over thirty shops _____ High Street.

k. The subject seems to be easy _____ the beginning.

l. They walked _____ the hotel.

m. He promised to call back _____ two hours.

n. It didn't happen today, but the day _____ yesterday.

o. If she doesn't get angry _____ the next hour, it will be ok.

p. I would like to know if you could make it _____ tonight.

q. Has anyone asked _____ me while I was away?

Übung 50
PRÄPOSITIONEN DES ORTES

a. The cat is sitting _____ (unter) the table.

b. We are going _____ (hinein) the house.

c. She walks _____ (hinunter) the stairs.

d. My car is parked _____ (links) of the road.

e. Tom is standing _____ (zwischen) Eddy and Rolf.

f. The picture is _____ (über) the door.

g. There were no pictures _____ (an) the wall.

h. He drove _____ (über) the bridge.

Übung 51
PRÄPOSITIONEN DER ZEIT

a. She was born _____ a Tuesday, _____ 1964.

b. My last haircut was three months _____.

c. _____ Easter, we will be in the snow.

d. I'm knackered, she woke me up _____ night.

e. You should cut the hedge _____ spring.

f. School finished _____ 11:30 today.

g. _____ New Year's Eve, Tom and Mary are coming.

h. Can we meet again _____ two weeks?

Übung 52
PHRASAL VERBS

a. My friend is good _____ playing football.

b. The customer complains _____ the fees.

c. The children are afraid _____ snakes.

d. She doesn't feel _____ working outside.

e. We are looking forward _____ meeting you soon.

f. He apologized _____ being late again.

g. The boys insisted _____ taking the car.

h. We stopped _____ in a hotel.

i. Who is taking _____ the position of the chairman?

j. The sign says you must keep _____ the lawn.

k. It took a while before the situation eased _____

l. If you look back _____ it, would you do it again?

m. Miriam drops _____ every day.

n. You better write it _____ before you forget it.

o. It's hot, why don't you take _____ your jumper?

p. All the hard work finally paid _____.

q. The situation is getting _____ hand.

r. This year, Easter coincides _____ my mom's birthday.

s. We have run _____ milk, could you get some please?

t. I cannot put _____ this guy any longer.

u. Who can do _____ a mobile phone today?

Konjunktionen

KONJUNKTIONEN sind Bindewörter, die Satzteile oder Satzglieder miteinander verbinden. Die meisten Konjunktionen machen keine Schwierigkeiten. Dies ist eine Auflistung und Anregung, das eine oder andere Bindewort öfter zu benutzen:

and	und	They liked the girl and the girl liked them.
but	aber	We wanted to visit the zoo, but it rained heavily.
or	oder	Would you like a cup of tea or rather a coffee?
however	wie auch immer/jedoch	I thought you would come home earlier, however, we can still go to the party.
whether	ob	Mum asks whether you are staying for dinner?
otherwise	andernfalls	Let's get going, otherwise it will be too late.
since	weil	We trust him since we know him.
in case	für den Fall, dass	In case we are not home, put the letter in the box.
even if	sogar wenn	She looks great, even if she wears old clothes.
even so	trotzdem	Even so he had studied, he got a bad mark.
in spite of	trotzdem	We will have a garden party in spite of the cold.
unless	wenn nicht	Unless you give in, we will not buy you an I-phone.

when	wenn (zeitlich)	You can call me when you get home.
although	obwohl	Although he knew us, he didn't even say hello.
yet	dennoch	The train was late, yet it didn't change her good mood.

Either, neither, or + nor

Either und neither werden von Ungeübten eher wenig verwendet. So geht es: Verwendet man in einem Satz eine Option mit „entweder–oder", muss es either–or heißen:

Either you take it or you leave it.
You can wear either the red dress or the black one.

Wenn zwei Dinge nicht eintreffen, also bei „weder–noch", verwendet man im Englischen neither–nor:

Neither Ruth nor Philipp were on time.
We met neither my father nor my mother at the party.

Either alleine steht auch für „einer von beiden".

Either of you two can have the ticket.
We take either of those shoes.

Either kann außerdem „auch nicht" heißen. Der Satz enthält dann immer eine Verneinung: Sie konnte *auch nicht* kommen.

She couldn't come to the party either.
He didn`t see the film either.

Neither steht für „keine/r von beiden". In einem solchen Satz kommt dann keine Verneinung mehr vor, die steckt bereits in neither:

Neither of them had got up early enough.
Neither of them could come to the party.

Gut zu wissen – good to know

Quid, quite, quiet

Klingt ähnlich, sieht ähnlich aus, bedeutet aber etwas völlig anderes:

TO QUIT   etwas aufgeben, aufhören

to quit a job, to quit smoking

Hier wird das I wie I ausgesprochen und das T am Ende wie ein T, nämlich stimmlos, hart. *KWIT*

QUID   Slang für die englische Währung Pfund

10 quid = £ 10

Hier wird das D am Ende auch wie ein D ausgesprochen, nämlich stimmhaft, weich. Das I bleibt I. *KWID*

QUIET   ruhig, still

quieter, the quietest

Hier wird das I wie EI ausgesprochen und das E ist hörbar: *KWEIET.*

QUITE   ziemlich

quite good

NOT QUITE nicht ganz

not quite middle England

Auch hier wird das I wie EI ausgesprochen, aber das E am Ende ist stumm: *KWEIT.*

Yesterday etc.

two weeks ago	vor zwei Wochen
the day before yesterday	vorgestern
yesterday	gestern
today	heute
tomorrow	morgen
the day after tomorrow	übermorgen
in a fortnight	in zwei Wochen
in one year's time	in einem Jahr

Nationalities

Die Nationalitäten verwenden wir nicht tagtäglich. Es gibt unterschiedliche Endungen, die häufigste ist -an:

NATIONALITÄT	LAND
jemand „ist"	Land
American	America
African	Africa
Austrian	Austria
Belgian	Belgium
Estonian	Estonia
German	Germany
Italian	Italy
Latvian	Latvia
Norwegian	Norway
Serbian	Serbia

Am zweithäufigsten kommt die Endung -sh vor:

British/English	Großbritannien/England
Danish	Denmark
Finnish	Finland
Irish	Ireland
Spanish	Spain
Swedish	Sweden

Andere Endungen:

French	-ch	France
Dutch		The Netherlands
Cypriot	-iot	Cyprus
Greek	-k	Greece
Iraqi	-i	Iraq
Israeli		Israel
Kuwaiti		Kuwait
Yemeni		Yemen

Lebanese	-ese	Lebanon
Portuguese		Portugal
Swiss	-ss	Switzerland

Slang

Im Sprachgebrauch jeder Sprache existiert Slang – Umgangssprache. Das ist gesprochene Sprache im Gegensatz zur Schriftsprache, die nicht gedruckt werden würde, da Slang grammatikalisch häufig nicht korrekt ist. Es gibt Slang-Wörter, aber auch Slang in der Grammatik, die man z. B. in Songtexten hört:

We roll outta …	out of
There ain't no sunshine.	is no
We're gonna give up.	going to
She do me no harm.	does
I wanna …	want to

Wo stehen Zeitangaben im Satz?

Zeitangaben stehen entweder am Satzanfang oder am Satzende, aber nicht in der Mitte. Ob man sie vorne oder hinten verwendet, verändert die Bedeutung des Satzes nicht.

Tomorrow I go shopping.
I go shopping tomorrow.
At the end of the week the furniture will arrive.
The furniture will arrive at the end of the week.

Often, usually, sometimes, always

Dies sind Häufigkeitsadverbien. Ihre Position ist in der Regel *vor dem Vollverb*:

He often forgets to put on his hat.
We usually go shopping on a Thursday.
I sometimes find it difficult to understand my teacher.
My father always orders the same meal at the restaurant.

Mehr Redewendungen

In for a penny, in for a pound.	Wer A sagt, muss auch B sagen.
First things first.	Eins nach dem anderen.
Garbage in, garbage out.	Von Nichts kommt nichts.
No pain, no gain.	Ohne Fleiß kein Preis.
Easy come, easy go.	Wie gewonnen, so zerronnen.
Out of sight, out of mind.	Aus den Augen, aus dem Sinn.
As thick as a brick.	Dumm wie Bohnenstroh.
Fortune favours fools.	Dumme haben immer Glück.
Any Tim, Dick or Harry.	Jeder Hinz und Kunz.
Tit for tat.	Wie du mir, so ich dir.
It's wishful thinking.	Wunschdenken

Confusing words – ähnliche Wörter

Bring + take

Diese Wörter werden oft verwechselt, weil beide „bringen" bedeuten. Aber es gibt unterschiedliche Anwendungen:

Bring wird verwendet, wenn man über den Empfänger einer Sache spricht, wenn also etwas *zu* jemandem „(mit)gebracht" wird.

Take wird verwendet, wenn man eine Sache oder Person *von sich weg* bringt. Take heißt auch „(weg/mit)nehmen":

Please bring me the paper, will you?	zu mir
You can take the paper with you if you want.	mitnehmen
Is she bringing a cake for the party?	mitbringen
Is she taking the cake to the party?	mitnehmen
Last year she only brought her children.	mitbringen
This year she took her children to the grandparents.	mitnehmen
Take the parcel and bring it home.	nimm/bring

Bring + take

Do und make bedeuten beide „machen", aber was passt wann? Die Faustregel besagt: Make wird verwendet, wenn etwas hergestellt wird. I made the cake. He made the cupboard. Grundsätzlich muss man lernen, wann do und wann make verwendet werden:

He has to do his homework straight after school.
In our house I do all the housework.
Do your job as good as you can!
He does everything for his mother.
He doesn't do any harm.
This company does market research.

She makes the beds every morning.
She always makes many mistakes in her exams.
You better make a shopping list.
I will make you a cup of coffee.
She makes all the arrangements for the wedding.
He makes a lot of money with his business.

Become + get

Become wird häufig mit „bekommen/erhalten" verwechselt, bedeutet aber „werden". „Bekommen/erhalten" auf Englisch ist to get:

You have become so selfish recently.	werden
I wonder what will become of her.	werden
What did you get for your birthday?	erhalten
We got five new children in our class.	bekommen
They are getting new furniture.	erhalten

Borrow + lend

Genauso schwierig sind diese beiden Vokabeln. Die eine heißt „ausleihen", die andere „verleihen". Es kommt also darauf an, ob der Sprecher etwas *nimmt* oder *gibt*.

Borrow bedeutet „ausleihen" (einfacher zu merken mit der Eselsbrücke „sich ausborgen") und meint immer, dass jemand etwas *nimmt*.
Lend dagegen bedeutet „verleihen", also jemandem etwas *geben*:

Can I borrow this book from you?	nehmen
You can't borrow it now I'm afraid,	nicht nehmen
but once I've finished it, I will lend it to you.	geben
My sister doesn´t lend her clothes to anyone.	nicht (her)geben

Large + big + tall

Für „groß" gibt es im Englischen viele Wörter.
Large wird eher verwendet für Flächen oder alles, was man füllen kann: The jumper is too large. This is a large house with a large garden. Is this box large enough?
Big dagegen betont eher die Masse, das Volumen. So sind dicke Menschen big: She is a big girl. This is a big apple. Es wird auch verwendet, wenn „älter und mächtiger" gemeint ist: He is my big brother. He has a big business.
Tall wird eher verwendet für alles, was lang ist und in die Höhe strebt, unter anderem für die Größe einer Person: I'm 1,78 m tall. How tall is the Eiffel Tower?
Mehr Beispiele:

This is a rather large forest we are in.	große Fläche
Their car is larger than ours.	viel Raum
You need a large/big dictionary.	umfangreich
I have got a big brother.	älter
He needs to take a big decision.	wichtig
She is a big girl.	korpulent
How tall are you?	Körpergröße
This tree is very tall.	hoch

Want + will

Want und will werden manchmal verwechselt, da man bei will an „ich will" denkt, also an das deutsche „wollen". Es gilt aber:

want = wollen, möchten (eher Wunsch)
will   = Zukunftsform von to be, meist im Sinne von
          „sicher tun werden" (eher Plan)

I want to get up early in the morning,	Wunsch
because I don't want to be late.	Wunsch
We will get up early in the morning,	Plan
so we won't be late.	Plan

When + if

When und if haben unterschiedliche Bedeutungen: When bedeutet „wenn/wann" und meint einen Zeitpunkt („wenn" im zeitlichen Sinne). If bedeutet „wenn/falls/ob" und beschreibt eine Bedingung oder eine Unsicherheit („wenn" im konditionalen Sinne):

I don't know when we are getting there.	wann
When we are at grandma's house could you	
please be a good girl!	wenn
I wonder if he will come.	ob
If she invites us, can you please say thank you!	falls

To + too

To ist eine Präposition und bedeutet „zu/bis" im raum-zeitlichen Sinne. Es wird kurz ausgesprochen:

I go to the doctor.	zum
From Monday to Friday	bis
To look up to	aufschauen zu

Achtung, nicht verwirren lassen: Das erste to in to look up to gehört im Englischen zum Infinitiv (to go, to speak, to understand) und hat keine eigene Bedeutung, es hat nur eine grammatische Funktion. Erst das zweite to ist die Präposition und bedeutet „zu". Das „zu" ohne eigene Bedeutung gibt es im Deutschen nur im sog. erweiterten Infinitiv (Er geht zur Schule, um zu lernen.)

Too fungiert als Adverb und hat die Bedeutung „zu" im Sinne von „zu sehr". Es wird lang ausgesprochen.

The problem was too severe to ignore it.   zu wichtig/ernst

I could tell she wasn't too pleased to meet us.   nicht sehr erfreut

Am Satzende bedeutet too außerdem „auch" und wird mit Komma abgetrennt:

This is very tricky, too.   auch

Praxis

Übung 53
DO oder MAKE?

a. Please, can you _____ me a favour?

b. If you _____ that again, you can go to bed now.

c. When I get up in the morning, I _____ the beds.

d. Can you please _____ the tea?

e. Every year we _____ a journey as a family.

f. He always _____ his best.

g. They _____ good headway with their project.

h. This doesn't _____ me any good.

Abschliessende Übungen

Diese drei abschließenden Übungen testen noch einmal das Sprachverständnis. Sie kommen in dieser Form in Cambridge-Tests vor.
Nutzen Sie die Gelegenheit die Vokabeln nachzuschlagen und die
richtige Lösung zu finden.

It's your turn
Übung 54

READING COMPREHENSION
One word (A, B, C or D) best completes each sentence:

1. We arrived _____ the airport four hours before our flight
   was due to leave.
   A in   B on   C at   D by

2. Anna is slowly getting used _____ the new machine.
   A to operate   B operating   C to operating   D for operate

3. The ambulance women administered first _____ on the
   spot.
   A help   B aid   C assistance   D treatment

4. Be careful you don't _____ your wallet!
   A loose   B lose   C to lose   D loosen

5. I'm afraid David hasn't got _____ his illness yet.
   A through   B up   C over   D out

6. Mary and Joe decided to go to the fancy _____ party as
   cooks.
   A costume   B clothes   C dress   D habit

7. Stephan knew many poems _____ heart.
   A with   B to   C from   D by

8. Susan _____ her mother in her love of gardening.

   A takes after   B looks like   C follows after   D stands by

Übung 55

USE OF ENGLISH

Fill only one word in each space.

a. _____ are many benefits to being a housecat: people give you food, people pet you and you have shelter when it rains or gets cold.

b. In many parts _____ the world, cats do not eat cat food the way it is made in the U.S.A.

c. _____ you ever been to Sea World?

d. Sea World is in San Diego, California. They have many marine animal exhibits and some _____ good shows.

e. In 1928 Amelia Earhart became famous as the first woman to fly from America to Europe. On _____ occasion she was a passenger.

f. But in 1932 _____ the age of thirty five,

g. she became the first woman to fly solo _____ the Atlantic.

h. In 1937 she decided to _____ again,

i. this _____ in the opposite direction.

Übung 56
ZEITEN IM TEXT BESTIMMEN

In each paragraph try to find, underline and name as many tenses as possible.

a. News that the Crown Estate returned record profits of £285m last year means the Queen is expected to receive a further £2m in public funding next year. But just how rich is the Queen and where does her wealth come from?

b. EU leaders holding late-night talks in Brussels have agreed to relocate tens of thousands of migrants who have arrived in Italy and Greece.

c. Austria and Germany are expecting more migrants to arrive, after thousands travelled from Hungary on Sunday following Budapest's easing of restrictions.

d. England striker Wayne Rooney described equalling Sir Bobby Charlton's scoring record as a "huge honour" after moving level with the World Cup winner on 49 goals for his country.

e. As the capital gears up to unveil this year's most exciting new product and furniture designs, here are our five favourites.

f. To end this crisis, we need more than grief. We need to see we're broken. It's emotional voyeurism when we fail to care beyond being sad for the victims of the tragedies that our government helped create and which we all ignored.

g. Shearling is a key trend this season. So there has never been a better time to invest in some robust outwear. Complement your jacket with loose jeans or a flannel shirt, or dress it up with a pair of sharp trousers and a turtleneck jumper.

h. The empty roads north of Madrid are perfect for this fun new group tour. And with great restaurants and atmospheric places to stay along the way, it gives a great flavor of the region, too.

Anhang

Englisch ist nicht gleich Englisch

In England ist im Oktober autumn, in Amerika dagegen fall. Ebenso wie in der Kultur beider Länder gibt es auch in Wortschatz, Aussprache und Schreibweise Unterschiede. Manche Wörter hat man unter Umständen in beiden Schreibweisen gesehen oder zwei Wörter für die gleiche Sache gehört. Das kann irreführend sein. Was ist korrekt? Die Antwort ist: Beide existieren nebeneinander. Welche Kultur und Schreib- oder Sprechweise jemand bevorzugt, wird davon abhängen, zu welcher Kultur man sich mehr hingezogen fühlt oder zu welcher man einen größeren Bezug hat. Es ist letztendlich Gewohnheit oder Geschmacksache und hängt davon ab, wo man lebt und welche Lehrer man hatte. An deutschen Schulen wird britisches Englisch gelehrt, viele Computerprogramme dagegen sind mit der amerikanischen Schreibweise voreingestellt. Viele Unternehmen haben eine Vorgabe, welche Version verwendet wird. Wichtig ist die Konsequenz: Innerhalb eines Textes oder einer Konversation muss (Schule, Uni, Prüfungen) oder sollte man sich für eine Schreib- oder Sprechweise entscheiden.

Unterschiedliches Vokabular (Beispiele)

BE (Britisch English)	AE (American English)	
Aubergine	egg plant	Aubergine
autumn	fall	Herbst
bank holiday	national holiday	Feiertag
barrister, solicitor	lawyer, attorney	Rechtsanwalt
to bath	to bathe	baden
bin, dustbin	garbage/trash can	Abfalleimer
boot	trunk	Kofferraum
braces	suspenders	Hosenträger
car park	parking lot	Parkplatz
chemistry	pharmacy	Apotheke
chips	French fries	Pommes Frites
city centre	downtown	Stadtzentrum
crisps	potato chips	Kartoffelchips
driving licence	driver's license	Führerschein
engaged	busy	besetzt (Telefon)
Father Christmas	Santa Claus	Weihnachtsmann
to fill in	to fill out	ausfüllen
fish-fingers	fish sticks	Fischstäbchen
flat	apartment	Wohnung
football	soccer	Fußball
fringe	bangs	Pony (Frisur)
garden	yard	Garten (Haus)
Gents	Men's Room	Herrentoilette
holiday	vacation	Urlaub
hoover	vacuum cleaner	Staubsauger
jacket potato	baked potato	Ofenkartoffel
Joe Bloggs	John Doe	Otto Normal
ladybird	ladybug	Marienkäfer

letter box	mail box	Briefkasten
lift	elevator	Aufzug
managing director	CEO	Generaldirektor
maths	math	Mathematik
mobile phone	cell phone	Handy
motorway	freeway, highway	Autobahn
mum	mom	Mutter
petrol	gas	Benzin
plane	airplane	Flugzeug
post(man)	mail(man)	Post(bote)
prawn	shrimp	Garnele
primary school	elementary school	Grundschule
to queue	to line up	anstehen
quid	buck	1 Pfund, 1 Dollar
railway	railroad	Eisenbahn
to ring	to call	anrufen
rubber	eraser	Radiergummi
share	stock	Aktie
shop	store	Laden
sweets	candies	Süßigkeiten
term	semester	Semester
tin	can	Dose
torch	flashlight	Taschenlampe
trousers	pants	Hose
tyre	tire	Reifen
underground, tube	subway	U-Bahn
year	grade	(Schul-) Klasse
zebra crossing	crosswalk	Fußgängerüberweg

Unterschiedliche Schreibweisen

Die Voreinstellungen der Schreibprogramme in Computern folgen dem Land der Herstellung des Produkts, aus diesem Grund ist es oftmals die amerikanische Schreibweise. Schreibt man dann Wörter auf englische Art, zeigt das Programm einen Fehler an – und andersherum.

BE (Britisch English)	AE (American English)	
Wörter auf -re	enden auf -er	
centre	center	Zentrum
theatre	theater	Theater
Wörter mit -ou	mit -o	
flavour	flavor	Geschmack, Aroma
colour	color	Farbe
Wörter auf -ogue	enden auf -og	
catalogue	catalog	Katalog
dialogue	dialog	Dialog
Wörter mit -s	mit -z	
cosy	cozy	gemütlich
organise	organize	organisiere
Wörter mit -ence	mit -ense	
licence	license	Erlaubnis
defence	defense	Verteidigung
Wörter mit -mme	mit -m	
programme	program	Programm

Unterschiedliche Aussprache

Das offensichtlichste Unterscheidungsmerkmal zwischen britischem und amerikanischem Englisch ist die Aussprache. Zusätzlich gibt es innerhalb jedes Landes regionale Akzente. Dem amerikanischen Englisch sagt man nach, es sei breiter. Britisches Englisch wird gerne als das „bessere" Englisch bezeichnet, amerikanisches als das „modernere". Jahrelang galt „Oxford-Englisch" als Maß aller Dinge – vergleichbar mit der Qualifizierung „Hochdeutsch". Immer häufiger spricht man heute vom BBC-Englisch und bezieht sich damit auf den größten britischen Nachrichtensender BBC. Recht sinnlos ist der Streit, ob amerikanisches Englisch schlechter oder besser sei, Fakt aber ist: Ein klares Oxford- oder BBC-Englisch ist für uns einfacher zu verstehen als amerikanisches, kanadisches oder australisches Englisch oder gar regionale Akzente, weshalb es sich zum Lernen besonders gut eignet.

Unterschiedliche Grammatik

HAVE/HAS GOT + DO YOU HAVE
Have got ist im Amerikanischen unüblich:
Die Amerikaner bevorzugen do you have.

Do you have time?	England auch: Have you got time?
Do they have a house?	England auch: Have they got a house?

TO GET
Die 3. FORM von to get lautet im Amerikanischen gotten:

BE	to get	got	got
AE	to get	got	gotten

She hasn't gotten over it.

PRESENT PERFECT + SIMPLE PAST
Im Amerikanischen kann für PRESENT PERFECT auch SIMPLE PAST verwendet werden – wo im britischen PRESENT PERFECT stehen MUSS:

BE	AE
I have just had supper.	I just had supper.
I have already been there.	I already was there.

ARE oder IS

Gruppen werden im britischen Englisch als Teams mit mehreren Mitgliedern interpretiert, deshalb steht das Verb meist im Plural, im amerikanischen Englisch steht das Verb im Singular, wenn auch das Subjekt im Singular steht (wie im Deutschen):

BE	AE
Our team are here to help.	Our team is here to help.
Meatloaf are in Paris.	Meatloaf is in Paris.

UNTERSCHIEDE IM BUSINESS-UMFELD

Einige Unterschiede existieren im Business English, beispielsweise für die Korrespondenz (auch Email) – die kursiven Stellen bedeuten: hier ist es bei BE und AE gleich.

BE

Datum	30 July 2014
Anrede Empfänger unbekannt	Dear Mr, Mrs – ohne Punkt
	Dear Sir, Dear Sirs, Dear Madam,
	to whom it may concern
Anrede Empfänger bekannt	*Dear, Hi, Hello John, Hi there, Hi all*
Satzzeichen nach Anrede	entweder nichts oder Komma
Abschluss Empfänger bekannt	*Sincerely yours, Yours sincerely* – ohne Komma
Abschluss Empfänger unbekannt	Faithfully yours, Yours faithfully – ohne Komma
Gruss in Emails	*Regards, Kind regards, Best wishes*
Lebenslauf	CV (Curriculum Vitae)

AE

Datum	July 30, 2014
Anrede Empfänger unbekannt	Dear Mr., Mrs. – mit Punkt
	Ladies and Gentlemen,
	to whom it may concern

Anrede Empfänger bekannt	*Dear, Hi, Hello John, Hi there, Hi all*
Satzzeichen nach Anrede	Doppelpunkt
Abschluss Empfänger bekannt	*Sincerely yours, Yours sincerely* – mit Komma
Abschluss Empfänger unbekannt	*Sincerely, Sincerely yours* – mit Komma
Gruss in Emails	*Regards, Kind regards, Best wishes*
Lebenslauf	Resume

Für beide Lebensläufe (BE + AE) gilt: keine Angaben über Geburts-ort, Familienstand und Religion, kein Foto.

Typisch Englisch

SMALL TALK

Engländer sind – im privaten und geschäftlichen Umfeld – in ihrer Art weniger direkt als wir Deutschen. Sie formulieren und äußern beispielsweise Kritik subtiler. Englische Manager (amerikanische ebenfalls) sehen sich oft als Vermittler und Motivator, im Gegensatz zu deutschen Führungskräften, für die Autorität häufig oberste Bedeutung hat. Außerdem hat small talk einen hohen Stellenwert. Er dient dazu, zu seinem Gegenüber erst einmal eine Beziehung aufzu-bauen und ein Gefühl für ihn zu entwickeln, was in Deutschland ger-ne vernachlässigt wird, wo man ein Thema schnell frontal angeht. Für Amerika und England gilt gleichermaßen: Höflichkeit wird viel und gerne ausgedrückt durch thank you und please.

DISCIPLINE

Queuing = Schlange stehen ist etwas, das die Engländer geduldig tun. Es wird nicht gedrängelt, sondern gewartet. Das wird jedem Deutschen bei einem Besuch in einer englischen Stadt sofort auffal-len: Der Einstieg in Busse ist vorne und man sieht lange Schlangen an den Haltestellen, einer hinter dem anderen.

HUMOUR

Eine der hervorstechendsten Eigenschaften der Engländer ist ihr Sinn für Humor und besonders die Fähigkeit, über sich selbst zu lachen. Die Mehrheit der Engländer nimmt sich nicht allzu ernst. Humoristen sind in England – in den USA übrigens auch – sehr hoch angesehen, viel höher als in Deutschland. Biersorten im Pub haben mitunter illustre Namen wie Pig's Ear und What he's having. Kaum vorstellbar, hierzulande eine Biersorte zu finden, die „Schweineohr" heißt bzw. „Für mich dasselbe". Humor wird in England auch durchaus im Geschäftsumfeld eingesetzt, um die Stimmung zu lockern oder eine gute Atmosphäre zu schaffen – etwas, wofür man in Deutschland schnell als „nicht ernsthaft" oder gar „nicht ernstzunehmen" abgestempelt werden kann.

OUTDOORS

Engländer sind ausgesprochene Naturliebhaber, sie lieben countryside und gardening. Das Besondere beim Wandern: Es gibt weitaus weniger begrenzte Wege, man darf nach Lust und Laune querfeldein gehen und muss häufig über cattle grids steigen oder durch Gatter gehen – in der Regel Abgrenzungen für Schafe. Bei einem Besuch in England lohnt es sich, einen der zahlreichen öffentlichen Gärten des National Trust zu besuchen.

PRIDE

Engländer sind stolz auf ihr Commonwealth – auch wenn es heute gar nicht mehr existiert. Europa ist gefühlt weit weg und wurde von den Briten schon immer als The Continent bezeichnet. Eine knappe Mehrheit der Engländer hat ganz aktuell ihr Gefühl von Unabhängigkeit zum Ausdruck gebracht – bei der Abstimmung über den Brexit mit einem Kreuz bei leave – und damit den Austritt aus der EU beschlossen.

PUB LIFE

Ebenfalls typisch englisch sind Teppichböden in den Pubs und dass man dort das Bier am Tresen kauft, sowie die Sperrstunde um 23 Uhr (last orders). Diese wurde zwar 2005 offiziell aufgehoben, aber noch viele Pubs praktizieren sie, da sie ein so fester Bestandteil der englischen Kultur ist.

ANGLIZISMEN

Unser Leben wird zunehmend von Computern bestimmt, und viele dieser Produkte kommen aus den USA. Jede Menge Ausdrücke sind aus diesem Umfeld bereits in den deutschen Sprachgebrauch übergegangen. Jedes Kind weiß, was „googeln", „whatsappen" oder „browsen" heißt. Viele englische Wörter sind fester Bestandteil unserer Sprache. Das wird von Kritikern bemängelt, ist jedoch, auch sprachhistorisch, ein völlig normaler Vorgang. Linguistisch wird beim Eindeutschen eine deutsche Grammatikregel auf ein englisches Wort angewendet, bei Verben wird zum Beispiel die deutsche Verbendung -en an das englische Verb einfach angehängt und ebenso wird das Verb flektiert:

to post = posten, ich poste, du postest etc.

BEISPIELE für ANGLIZISMEN

Aftershave	ausloggen	Baby	Backoffice	Beauty
Bestseller	Bodybuilding	Business	Camping	chillen
CD	Couch	Date	einloggen	Food
Frisbee	Gameboy	Grapefruit	Handy	Hardware
Joggen	Kanu	Label	Management	Stylen
Tablet	(Coffee) to go	Training	uploaden	Wellness

Abschließend

Englisch ist die Muttersprache von etwa 330 Millionen Menschen weltweit, weitere mehrere hundert Millionen Menschen sprechen Englisch als Zweitsprache. In Deutschland wird Englisch im Arbeitsumfeld in vielen Berufen vorausgesetzt. Durch das deutsche Schulsystem haben viele Menschen in Deutschland sehr solide Englischkenntnisse. Allen, die sich verbessern wollen, hilft dieses Buch hoffentlich dabei, ihre Lücken zu schließen und Unklarheiten auszuräumen. Außerdem soll es dazu anregen, die englische Sprache mit Spaß anzuwenden.

Den letzten Schritt zu gutem Englisch macht ein Lernender allein durch das Anwenden. Wichtig ist es dabei, sich von deutschen Satzstrukturen zu lösen. Englische Sätze funktionieren am besten in klaren und einfachen Aussagen – also weg von verschachtelten Gedanken und hin zu geradlinigen Strukturen. Noch ein Tipp ist, möglichst in aktiven Sätzen zu formulieren, das ist am Anfang einfacher und kommt der Praxis näher als die Verwendung des Passivs. Außerdem sind Substantivierungen im Englischen wesentlich seltener als im Deutschen. Abschließend: Es gibt immer mehr als eine Möglichkeit, etwas auszudrücken. Will eine Formulierung nicht gleich funktionieren, versuchen Sie es auf andere Weise, Hauptsache: You (can) say it in English!

Lösungen zu den **Übungen**

Hinweis zu den Lösungen – diese Lösungen sind Vorschläge, die m. E. am besten passen – an der einen oder anderen Stelle mag alternativ auch mal eine andere Vokabel passen, ich verzichte aber darauf, alle möglichen Vokabeln anzuführen.

Übung 1
SÄTZE BILDEN MIT SIMPLE PRESENT (S. 41)

a. The bread looks tasty/nice.
b. He does not (doesn't) want to eat unless I feed him.
c. Don't they play chess every Wednesday/on a Wednesday?
d. He knows many poems by heart.
e. Does your mother sometimes forget anything?
f. What/which book does he like best?
g. How do you like my new haircut/hairdo?

Übung 2
MIT BE + HAVE (S. 41)

a. On Mondays the children are at school until half past one.
b. She is never on time.
c. She has (got) a BMW and a Porsche in her garage.
d. We are already happy when the sun is shining.
e. My father has (got) two brothers and five sisters.
f. Am I (really) so late?
g. Have you (got) / Do you have time for an old fool like me?
h. They are not happy / content with what they have (got) / they've got.

Übung 3
FRAGEN STELLEN mit und ohne FRAGEWORT (S. 42)

a. Is she from New York?
b. Does she meet her friend later?
c. Do we have two dogs now?

d. Are your names/are you Ann & Cathy?

e. Do they (the two) like chess?

f. When do you play tennis?

g. Why doesn't she have a husband?

Übung 4

SIMPLE PRESENT S ODER NICHT? (S. 43)

live / visit / does not (doesn't) live / lives / is not (isn't) / does not (doesn't) go / has (got) / am / is able / wants

Übung 5

SÄTZE im PRESENT CONTINUOUS BILDEN (S. 51)

a. They are sitting in the garden right now/at the moment/now.

b. We are running because the bus is coming.

c. I am not phoning at the moment. I am not on the phone.

d. In the picture we are standing in front of the cathedral.

e. At the moment she is doing nothing. She is doing nothing at the moment.

f. Quiet! You are making a lot of noise!

g. How are you feeling?

h. Look! The birds are drinking the water.

Übung 6

-ING ODER NICHT? (S. 52)

a. I think the new colleague is rather/quite nice.

b. She is caring for her mother.

c. I do care about how you feel/how you are feeling, you know!

d. Do you believe in anything?

e. This means a lot to us.

f. In this case it doesn't matter.

g. They don't believe that he is writing the exam right now.

h. I am only just realising that you are hurt.

Übung 7

SÄTZE BILDEN MIT PRESENT PERFECT + CONTINUOUS (S. 67)

a. We have only moved here recently.
b. It's 11 o'clock and she still hasn't got up yet.
c. I haven't seen her since yesterday.
d. We haven't booked a holiday this year.
e. We have been to Canada three times already.
f. Have you saved me some lunch?
g. How long / Since when have you been working for Paul?
h. We have been cruising for three weeks in the Mediterranean Sea.

Übung 8

WAS PASST? UNTERSTREICHEN: PRESENT PERFECT oder CONTINUOUS? (S. 67)

a. have known/told
b. both possible
c. have seen/has been working
d. have been telling/have gone
e. have had
f. both possible/have heard
g. have spoken/both possible
h. Have you seen

Übung 9

WAS PASST? UNTERSTREICHEN: SIMPLE PRESENT/PRESENT PERFECT (S. 68)

a. cycles
b. has been driving
c. go
d. has been living
e. has played
f. practices

g. have known

h. comforts

Übung 10

EINSETZEN: PRESENT PERFECT oder PRESENT PERFECT
CONTINUOUS (S. 69)

a. have been calling/have you been

b. have been tidying

c. Have you found/have been looking

d. haven't discovered/haven't been looking/have just come

e. haven't cooked/have been talking

f. Have you had/have had

g. has been watching

h. have been cleaning/have told

Übung 11

SÄTZE ERWEITERN MIT PRESENT PERFECT (S. 70)

a. I have loved her since I met her.

b. She has been living on her own since her husband died.

c. He has been confined to a wheelchair since he had an accident.

d. We have been living here for three months.

e. How long has she had a cat?

f. She has put much effort in since she got the order.

g. He has seen the doctor regularly since his daughter told him to.

h. You have missed me since I left.

Übung 12

SIMPLE PAST SÄTZE BILDEN (S. 82)

a. When did the last meeting take place?

b. Didn't you spend last summer on the Maldives?

c. I was nineteen when I finished school.

d. Friends of ours moved to the USA at the beginning of the year.

e. We ordered our new car two weeks ago.

f. The house broke down during the last storm.

g. Yesterday Sarah decided to sell the house.

h. We visited our parents last week.

i. She was here a minute ago.

j. In former times time went by more quickly.

Übung 13

RICHTIGE VERBFORM EINSETZEN – SIMPLE PAST (S. 83)

a. existed/were/were/supported/got

b. Did you think/came

c. was not (wasn't)/won

d. got/took/sneaked/did not (didn't) catch/were

e. were/had to/were not (weren't)/were/found/did not (didn't) harm

f. did you do/chilled/went on

g. Did you know/was not (wasn't)/was

h. did not (didn't) say

Übung 14

SIMPLE PAST oder PRESENT PERFECT (S. 86)

a. Your parcel has arrived.

b. Have you seen my ballpoint?

c. Our neighbour had an accident three months ago.

d. She signed the contract at the end of the last season.

e. Your parcel arrived this morning.

f. Peter knew many poems by heart.

g. Charles Dickens lived in the 19th century.

h. A huge wave has broken the ship in two.

i. How long have you been reading the book?

j. He has been selected/chosen.

Übung 15

SIMPLE PRESENT oder PRESENT PERFECT CONTINUOUS (S. 87)

a. plays
b. has been driving
c. go
d. has been living
e. practices
f. have been waiting

Übung 16

PRESENT PERFECT CONTINUOUS BILDEN (S. 88)

a. The passengers have been waiting for the bus since the plane landed.
b. Have you been living in this house for a long time?
c. You have been tinkering with the car for ages.
d. We have been seeing Dr. Scott for years.
e. For an hour the class has been writing a test.
f. The noise has been going on for hours.
g. They have been playing in their room since this morning.
h. The rumours have been going on for months.

Übung 17

SÄTZE BILDEN mit PAST PERFECT (S. 95)

a. spent/had met
b. had done/picked up
c. showed/had hurt
d. looked/had sent
e. read/had recommended
f. hadn't touched
g. won/hadn't played
h. left/hadn't had

Übung 18
PRESENT PERFECT oder PAST PERFECT (S. 96)
a. We have only just arrived. (PRESENT)
b. We had only just left. (PAST)
c. I had seen him before. (PAST)
d. Have you finished vacuuming already? (PRESENT)
e. I've had enough of this! (PRESENT)
f. I'd just had enough. (PAST)
g. I hadn't seen that before. (PAST)
h. We've had an argument. (PRESENT)

Übung 19
SIMPLE PAST oder PAST PERFECT (S. 97)
a. built
b. had got
c. had left
d. caught
e. hadn't thought
f. started
g. caught
h. had already put

Übung 20
SÄTZE BILDEN im PAST PERFECT (S. 97)
a. had not touched
b. hadn't had
c. had given
d. had had
e. Had he spoken

Übung 21
SÄTZE BILDEN IM PAST CONTINUOUS (S. 103)
a. As soon as the sun came/was out the snowman was melting.
b. During their excursion, they were exploring new territories.
c. While she was on the phone, the secretary was printing out a document.
d. The girls were not concentrating on the task.
e. When mother came home, David wasn't practicing the piano.
f. During the show, Jill was dancing.
g. Your cousins were swimming in the lake when it started to rain.
h. During a visit the professor was answering the students' questions.

Übung 22
SÄTZE mit FUTURE bilden (S. 122)
a. Next week we are visiting/we are going to visit my great-aunt in Bavaria.
b. I will call you as soon as I get the files.
c. Where will you work in ten years time?
d. When does the film start?
e. Will anyone come to the Chinese restaurant?
f. We are driving down south tomorrow after breakfast.
g. What are you going to do after your apprenticeship/training?
h. Do you know what I am doing on Tuesday? I am collecting/ picking up my car.

Übung 23
PASSENDE FUTURE-FORM EINSETZEN (S. 123)
a. will call (unsicher, spontan)
b. is he arriving/does he arrive (sicher/time table)
c. retires (hier: Fahrplan)
d. will need (Vorhersage)
e. is going to throw (etwas kommen sehen)

f. I will be lying (wird dann passieren)

g. I am sending/am going to send (fest geplant)

h. going to have/having (locker/fest geplant)

Übung 24
RICHTIG EINSETZEN (S. 123)

a. we will be having

b. I am leaving

c   are you going to buy

d. leaves

e. will call

f. Are you seeing

g. I will be working

h. I am going to do

Übung 25
CONDITIONAL I, II oder III? (S. 132)

a. don't change

b. would you do

c. run out

d. would not be

e. will not be

f. had worn

g. will celebrate

h. had known

Übung 26
SÄTZE BILDEN mit CONDITIONAL (S. 133)

a. I will get really cross if you don't come here immediately/at once.

b. Had I listened to you back then, I would have had a better time.

c. Just imagine if we had that much money, what would we do?

d. We'll go to the party if there is food.

e. If he wasn't so violently tempered, he would be nice to work with.
f. The company would not have survived if it hadn't been listed (on the stock market).
g. If you let it ring three times I will know it's you.
h. If the garden was bigger we would have much more to do.

Übung 27
SÄTZE im CONDITIONAL BILDEN (S. 134)
a. is/will offer
b. were/would not (wouldn't) complain
c. had known/would/could have sent
d. will go/get
e. would be/won

Übung 28
DEKLINIEREN: Wir wohnen in Hamburg. (S. 136)

SIMPLE PRESENT	We live in Hamburg.
PRESENT CONTINUOUS	We are living in Hamburg.
PRESENT PERFECT	We have lived in Hamburg.
PRESENT PERFECT CONTINUOUS	We have been living in Hamburg.
SIMPLE PAST	We lived in Hamburg.
PAST PERFECT	We had lived in Hamburg.
PAST PERFECT CONTINUOUS	We had been living in Hamburg.
PAST CONTINUOUS	We were living in Hamburg.
FUTURE WILL	We will live in Hamburg.
FUTURE GOING TO	We are going to live in Hamburg.
FUTURE CONTINUOUS	We are living in Hamburg.
FUTURE SIMPLE PRESENT	We live in Hamburg.
CONDITIONAL I	If we want, we will live in Hamburg.

CONDITIONAL II   If we wanted, we would live
                                      in Hamburg.
CONDITIONAL III   If we had wanted, we would
                                      have lived.

Übung 29

DEKLINIEREN: Er mag Tiere. (S. 137)
SIMPLE PRESENT   He likes animals.
PRESENT CONTINUOUS   He is liking animals.
PRESENT PERFECT   He has liked animals.
PRESENT PERFECT
   CONTINUOUS   He has been liking animals.
SIMPLE PAST   He liked animals.
PAST PERFECT   He had liked animals.
PAST PERFECT
   CONTINUOUS   He had been liking animals.
PAST CONTINUOUS   He was liking animals.
FUTURE WILL   He will like animals.
FUTURE GOING TO   He is going to like animals.
FUTURE CONTINUOUS   He is liking animals.
FUTURE SIMPLE PRESENT He likes animals.
CONDITIONAL I   If he can, he will like animals.
CONDITIONAL II   If he could, he would like animals.
CONDITIONAL III   If he had been able to,
                                      he would have liked …

Übung 30

DEKLINIEREN: Das ist einfach. (S. 138)
SIMPLE PRESENT   This is easy.
PRESENT CONTINUOUS   This is being easy.
PRESENT PERFECT   This has been easy.
PRESENT PERFECT
   CONTINUOUS   This has been being easy.

SIMPLE PAST	This was easy.
PAST PERFECT	This had been easy.
PAST PERFECT	
CONTINUOUS	This had been being easy.
PAST CONTINUOUS	This was being easy.
FUTURE WILL	This will be easy.
FUTURE GOING TO	This is going to be easy.
FUTURE CONTINUOUS	This is being easy.
FUTURE SIMPLE PRESENT	This is easy.
CONDITIONAL I	If you look at it, it will be easy.
CONDITIONAL II	If you looked at it, it would be easy.
CONDITIONAL III	If you had looked at it,
	it would have been easy.

Übung 31

MIT THE ODER OHNE? (S. 149)

a. —/the (beides möglich)

b. the

c. the, the, —

d. —

e. the, the/— (beides möglich)

f. beides möglich

g. the, the

h. the

Übung 32

MIT THE oder A/AN oder OHNE? (S. 150)

a. Last year we spent the winter on/in the Maldives.

b. The school Karl goes to closes in (the) summer for three weeks.

c. The Müllers live in High Street, number 12.

d. Germany has only got one high mountain – the Zugspitze.

e. He is a car mechanic.

f. She is Portuguese/a Portuguese person.

g. Corfu is an island in the Ionic Sea.

h. Do you remember the Monday (when) you were fired?

Übung 33

RICHTIG EINSETZEN (S. 157)

a. anywhere

b. some

c. any

d. something

e. anyone/anybody

f. anybody/anything

g. somewhere

h. anybody/anyone

Übung 34

SÄTZE BILDEN mit MUCH, MANY, LITTLE, (A) FEW (S. 158)

a. I still know many friends from my former schooldays.

b. How much courage is needed to do bungee jumping!

c. Jacob has eaten so little today!

d. We have only not been to sports a few times.

e. There already were quite a few people.

f. There was little traffic on the roads today.

g. We went many times to their house for a meal.

h. Much ado about nothing.

Übung 35

mit USED TO (S. 161)

a. used to read

b. used to live

c. can't get used to working

d. got used to living

e. Did/use to

f. am used to getting up

g. used to be
h. used to visit

Übung 36
SÄTZE mit MUST, MUST NOT, HAD TO bilden (S. 163)

a. A football team must not have more than eleven players on the field.
b. During a football match the ball must not be stopped with the arm.
c. The players must play with the foot.
d. Substituted players mustn't be substituted again.
e. The rules must be obeyed.
f. Most children had to wait at the entrance to/in front of the swimming pool.
g. Generally, they must not go in without the teacher.
h. The bus had to wait at the bus stop because the doors would not close.

Übung 37
GERUNDIUM (S. 167)

a. I suggest meeting at 10 pm.
b. She insisted on driving to the meeting point herself.
c. We carry on doing as we have so far.
d. It doesn't help fussing about it.
e. How about going to the theatre together?
f. We dislike arguing.
g. He is famous for writing good books.
h. She enjoys painting very much.
i. We are very keen on travelling to Australia. / We would very much like travelling …

Übung 38
GERUNDIUM oder nicht? (S. 168)

a. not going

b. to get

c. smoking

d. to be

e. having

f. to see

g. to play / playing

h. leaving

Übung 39
ADJEKTIVE + ADVERBIEN (S. 175)

a. briefly

b. high

c. more interesting

d. delicious/tasty/nice

e. nicely

f. greatest

g. as good as

h. highly recommended

Übung 40
ADJEKTIVE + ADVERBIEN (S. 175)

a. not fast/soon enough

b. much better

c. well

d. carefully

e. angrily

f. cheap / reasonable

g. much more expensive

h. happily

Übung 41
SÄTZE MIT MODALVERBEN BILDEN (S. 179)
a. She had to stay longer.
b. Were you allowed to go to the cinema yesterday?
c. He mustn't fall asleep now.
d. He wasn't supposed to eat up everything.
e. It might be, that we will start later today. / Maybe we will …
f. You needn't wait for us.
g. You shouldn't miss this.
h. We would very much like to watch it with you.

Übung 42
ERSATZFORMEN von MODALVERBEN einsetzen (S. 180)
a. are supposed to
b. was able to
c. are allowed to
d. don't have to. have to
e. have to
f. are not allowed to
g. are not supposed to
h. are expected to

Übung 43
IN VERGANGENHEIT (SIMPLE PAST) SETZEN (S. 181)
a. Thomas <u>had to</u> tidy his office because he <u>couldn't</u> find anything.
b. His mother <u>told</u> him he <u>was expected to</u> be tidier.
c. You <u>were not allowed to</u> keep us waiting.
d. If the work <u>was</u> not good enough, he <u>didn't have to</u> panic.
e. The lady <u>was able to / could</u> help in the kindergarten.

Übung 44
WHO, WHICH, THAT oder OHNE? (S. 186)
a. which/that – oder ohne

b. which/that – oder ohne

c. who

d. who

e. which

f. which

g. who/that

h. which/that

Übung 45
SÄTZE VERBINDEN MIT WHO, WHOM, WHOSE oder WHICH (S. 187)

a. She is a hairdresser <u>who</u> has no job at the moment.

b. Tim is a musician <u>who(m)</u> I saw at a festival.

c. Dad got the letter <u>which/that</u> I sent from Spain last week.

d. This is the exam <u>which/that</u> I find very difficult.

e. This is our neighbour <u>whose</u> wife ran off.

f. Thomas, <u>who</u> lives next door, won the lottery.

g. They came to my party, <u>which/that</u> was very kind of them.

h. The meal, <u>which</u> we enjoyed, was delicious.

Übung 46
SÄTZE BILDEN im PASSIV (S. 190)

a. The politician was asked for an interview.

b. After all, the project can be financed.

c. The new novel is (being) praised by the reviewers.

d. The building works can be completed on Saturday.

e. The battery needs to be replaced.

f. The whole exam has to be repeated.

g. The manager should have been informed about the problem.

h. We are all invited to Maria's party.

Übung 47
PASSIVSÄTZE BILDEN in richtiger ZEIT (S. 191)
a. My car has been broken into.
b. The group was seen in the park.
c. The curtain is going to be hung up at the weekend.
d. The inline skates had been used before.
e. The museum will be closed.
f. Susan was told to give up smoking.
g. The table will be laid.
h. The book has been given to me.

Übung 48
SÄTZE BILDEN im AKTIV und PASSIV (S. 192)
a. Grapes grow in California. Grapes are grown in California.
b. The child washes itself. The child is washed.
c. The group gives up. The group is given up.
d. The little boy hits the big one. The little boy is hit by the big one.
e. The police saw the thief. The police were seen by the thief.

Übung 49
PRÄPOSITION EINSETZEN (S. 206)
a. at
b. after
c. at/on
d. in
e. on
f. by / at
g. of
h. in/by
i. at
j. in
k. in

l. to/towards

m. in / within

n. before

o. in/within

p. by

q. for

Übung 50
PRÄPOSITIONEN DES ORTES (S. 207)

a. under

b. into

c. down

d. on the left

e. between

f. above

g. on

h. over/across

Übung 51
PRÄPOSITIONEN DER ZEIT (S. 208)

a. on, in

b. ago

c. at

d. at

e. in

f. at

g. on

h. in

Übung 52
PHRASAL VERBS (S. 208)

a. at

b. about

c. of

d. like

e. to

f. for

g. on

h. over

i. over/on

j. off

k. off

l. on / at

m. in/by

n. down

o. off

p. off

q. out of

r. with

s. out of

t. up with

u. without

Übung 53

DO oder MAKE? (S. 219)

a. do

b. do

c. make

d. make

e. make

f. does

g. are making

h. do

Übung 54
READING COMPREHENSION (S. 220)
1. C
2. C
3. B
4. B
5. C
6. C
7. D
8. A

Übung 55
USE OF ENGLISH (S. 221)
a. There
b. of
c. Have
d. very/really
e. that
f. at
g. across/over
h. try/start
i. time

Übung 56
ZEITEN IM TEXT FINDEN + BESTIMMEN (S. 222)
a. <u>returned</u> SIMPLE PAST <u>means</u> SIMPLE PRESENT <u>is expected</u>
   PASSIVE <u>is/does come</u> SIMPLE PRESENT
b. <u>holding</u> PRESENT CONTINUOUS <u>have agreed/have arrived</u>
   PRESENT PERFECT
c. <u>are expecting</u> PRESENT CONTINUOUS <u>travelled</u> SIMPLE PAST
d. <u>described</u> SIMPLE PAST <u>moving</u> GERUNDIUM
e. <u>gears up</u> SIMPLE PRESENT <u>are</u> SIMPLE PRESENT

f. <u>need</u> MODALVERB <u>It's</u> SIMPLE PRESENT <u>being sad</u> PRESENT CONTINUOUS <u>ignored</u> SIMPLE PAST

g. <u>is</u> SIMPLE PRESENT <u>has never been</u> PRESENT PERFECT <u>Complement/dress it up</u> IMPERATIVE

h. <u>are/gives</u> SIMPLE PRESENT